The New Age Diet

VEGETARIANISM
FOR YOU AND ME

Published by:
GITA PUBLISHING HOUSE
Sadhu Vaswani Mission,
10, Sadhu Vaswani Path, Pune- 411 001, (India).
gph@sadhuvaswani.org

FOR PRIVATE CIRCULATION ONLY

The New Age Diet
Vegetarianism for You and Me
© **2012, J.P. Vaswani**
ISBN: 978-93-80743-56-1

DADA VASWANI'S BOOKS
Visit us online to purchase books on self-improvement,
spiritual advancement, meditation and philosophy. Plus audio
cassettes, CDs, DVDs, monthly journals and books in Hindi.
www.dadavaswanisbooks.org

Printed by:
MEHTA OFFSET PVT. LTD.
Mehta House,
A-16, Naraina Industrial Area II, New Delhi-110 028, (India).
info@mehtaoffset.com

The New Age Diet
VEGETARIANISM
FOR YOU AND ME

J.P. VASWANI

GITA PUBLISHING HOUSE
PUNE, (INDIA).
www.dadavaswanisbooks.org

Books and Booklets by Dada J.P. Vaswani

In English:
10 Commandments of a Successful Marriage
108 Pearls of Practical Wisdom
108 Simple Prayers of a Simple Man
108 Thoughts on Success
114 Thoughts on Love
A Little Book of Life
A Little Book of Wisdom
A Simple and Easy Way To God
A Treasure of Quotes
Around The Camp Fire
Begin the Day with God
Bhagavad Gita in a Nutshell
Burn Anger Before Anger Burns You
Comrades of God - Lives of Saints from East & West
Daily Appointment with God
Daily Inspiration (A Thought For Every Day Of The Year)
Daily Inspiration
Destination Happiness
Dewdrops of Love
Does God Have Favorites?
Finding Peace of Mind
Formula for Prosperity
Gateways to Heaven
God In Quest of Man
Good Parenting
How to Overcome Depression
I am a Sindhi
I Luv U, God!
In 2012 All Will Be Well!
Joy Peace Pills
Kill Fear Before Fear Kills You
Ladder of Abhyasa
Lessons Life Has Taught Me
Life after Death
Life and Teachings of Sadhu Vaswani
Life and Teachings of the Sikh Gurus: Ten Companions of God
Living in the Now
Management Moment by Moment
Mantras For Peace Of Mind
Many Paths: One Goal
Nearer, My God, To Thee!
New Education Can Make the World New
Peace or Perish: There Is No Other Choice
Positive Power of Thanksgiving
Questions Answered
Saints For You and Me

Saints With A Difference
Say No to Negatives
Secrets of Health And Happiness
Seven Commandments of the Bhagavad Gita
Shake Hands With Life
Short Sketches of Saints Known & Unknown
Sketches of Saints Known & Unknown
Stop Complaining: Start Thanking!
Swallow Irritation Before Irritation Swallows You
Teachers are Sculptors
The Goal Of Life and How To Attain It
The Little Book of Freedom from Stress
The Little Book of Prayer
The Little Book of Service
The Little Book of Success
The Little Book of Yoga
The Magic of Forgiveness
The Perfect Relationship: Guru and Disciple
The Terror Within
The Way of Abhyasa (How To Meditate)
Thus Have I Been Taught
Tips For Teenagers
What You Would Like To know About Karma
What You Would Like To know About Hinduism
What to Do When Difficulties Strike: 8 easy Practical Suggestions.
Why Do Good People Suffer?
You Are Not Alone: God Is With You!
You Can Change Your Life: Live— Don't Just Exist!
Why Be Sad

Story Books:
101 Stories For You And Me
25 Stories For Children and also for Teens
It's All A Matter of Attitude
Snacks For The Soul
More Snacks For The Soul
Break The Habit
The Heart of a Mother
The King of Kings
The Lord Provides
The One Thing Needful
The Patience of Purna

The Power of Good Deeds
The Power of Thought
Trust Me All in All or Not at All
Whom Do You Love the Most?
You Can Make A Difference
100 Stories You Will Never Forget
The Miracle of Forgiving

In Hindi:
Aalwar Santon Ki Mahan Gaathaayen
Aapkay Karm, Aapkaa Bhaagy Banaatay Hein
Atmik Jalpaan
Atmik Poshan
Bhakton Ki Uljhanon Kaa Saral Upaai
Bhale Logon Ke Saath Bura Kyon?
Chaahat Hai Mujhe Ik Teri Teri
Dainik Prerna
Dar Se Mukti Paayen
Ishwar Tujhe Pranam
Krodh Ko Jalayen Swayam Ko Nahin
Laghu Kathayein
Mrityu Hai Dwar... Phir Kya?
Prarthana ki Shakti
Sadhu Vaswani: Unkaa Jeevan Aur Shikshaayen
Safal Vivah Ke Dus Rahasya
Santon Ki Leela
Srimad Bhagavad Gita: Gaagar Mein Saagar

In Marathi:
Jyachya Jholeet Aahay Prem Karm
Krodhaver Vijay Milva
Mrityu Nantarche Jeevan
Yashashvi Vaivahik Jeevanachi Sutray

Other Publications:

Books on Dada J. P. Vaswani:
A Pilgrim of Love
Dada J.P. Vaswani's Historic Visit to Sind
Dost Thou Keep Memory
How To Embrace Pain
Interviews and Inner views
Jiski Jholi Mein Hain Pyaar
Life and Teachings of Dada J.P. Vaswani
Living Legend
Moments with a Master
Pyar Ka Masiha

Author's Preface

As a humble pilgrim on the path, I have been offered the opportunity to meet with several fellow seekers and travelers on the highway of life. Wherever life has taken me, wherever I have travelled, I have learnt valuable lessons, gained valuable insights from my brothers and sisters, my fellow pilgrims. In return, I have shared with them the wisdom of ancient India, the wisdom of our great *rishis* and the deathless culture that is our heritage as children of this great land. Above all, I have taken the greatest pleasure, and deemed it my priceless privilege to carry to the people, the message of my Master, the treasure of the wisdom that has been left to us by Gurudev Sadhu Vaswani, a great soul unparalleled for its matchless splendor on India's spiritual firmament.

I truly believe that these lips of mine are unworthy to lisp his name, and yet it is my life's mission, the purpose of this God given existence upon this earth, to carry his message to as many people as I can, in as many ways as I can, with as much effect and power that I am capable of! Whatever I know, whatever I write, whatever I speak and any good that I may have done to others, has been through the grace of my Guru. Rarely do I speak or write, without acknowledging the deep gratitude that I owe to my Gurudev, this great saint, the beloved son of this land, who was a sage and seer in the tradition of our ancient *rishis*. Every utterance of mine begins with a tribute to my Gurudev; and every discourse includes an exhortation to the audience to imbibe one of his most cherished ideals: the golden rule of the sanctity of all life and the need to practice, in deeds of daily life, the ideal of Reverence for all life.

In simple, practical terms, this is an appeal to all brothers and sisters to adopt the principle of Vegetarianism. This book is no exception to the rule!

This deep awareness of the need for reverence for all life formed a very essential part of Gurudev Sadhu Vaswani's teachings and has been propagated emphatically by the Sadhu Vaswani Mission. In 1986, we inaugurated the International Meatless Day Campaign, which seeks to initiate an awareness of reverence for all forms of life by appealing to the people to abstain from all food of violence, on November 25, Gurudev Sadhu Vaswani's Birthday. The Sadhu Vaswani Mission is also committed to the building of a new world order based on the principle of non-violence and reverence for all life. To this end, we have established the SAK–Stop All Killing Association based on the philosophy expounded by Gurudev Sadhu Vaswani, who is hailed as a Prophet of Compassion and a modern day Saint. The aim of the SAK Association is:

- To create and foster reverence for all life, in the belief that ALL life must be regarded as sacred, for this is the first step towards World Peace.

- To work towards drafting a charter of Animal Rights.

- To create a belief in the Brotherhood of all Life.

- To promote and propagate the practice of vegetarianism.

To this end, we have been celebrating Gurudev Sadhu Vaswani's Birthday, November 25, as World Animal Rights and Meatless Day. It is our hope that the token observation of Meatless Day and Animal Rights Day will eventually sow the seeds of a totally vegetarian way of life in the minds of many. Gurudev Sadhu Vaswani's spirit, I believe, speaks through my weak words when I tell my listeners with undying emphasis: The time has come when we must decide, once and for all, that all types of human exploitation must cease. We must recognise the moral inviolability of individual life – both human and non-human. Just as one race of people cannot exist as resources for another, even so, animals cannot continue to exist as resources for human beings!

Sometimes, friends and well wishers say to me, not without a trace of embarrassment, "Dada, we are amazed that you have the courage to stand up before a mixed audience of a few vegetarians and a vast majority of non-vegetarians, and appeal to all of them to refrain from flesh food! How do you do it? We have heard about what is called the courage of conviction; but aren't you afraid of courting unpopularity, of offending people's sentiments when you raise your voice against the food of violence?"

I say to them with a smile, "How can any offence be taken when no offence is meant? Is it not a good thing that we share with our friends the best that we have and hold? And besides, what I hold up before them is not a personal whim of mine. It is the essence of India's ancient wisdom, the essence of the *Vedas*.

For it is *Vedanta* that teaches us that there is but One Life in all. The One Life sleeps in the mineral and the stone, stirs in the vegetable and the plant, dreams in the animal and wakes up in man. Creation is one family and birds and animals are man's younger brothers and sisters in this beautiful family. Is it not then, our duty to guard our younger brothers and sisters from the cruel knife of the butcher?"

To the readers of this book, let me say: I do not apologise for my dearly held beliefs. No offence is meant when I plead the cause of vegetarianism. I am convinced, on the contrary, that it is the right choice of diet, indeed, the diet of the future, for a happy, healthy, harmonious life for all humanity!

Dear readers, you would all agree with me when

I say, these are troubled times, indeed turbulent times that we live in. Insensate violence and strife are all-pervasive. Murder, mayhem, corruption and cruelty have become the norm of 'news' content to which we listen daily, too numbed even to react. Very occasionally, we revolt in horror, only to relapse into our habitual apathy. But beneath the veneer of indifference, beneath the numbed response to the violence, there is the despair of the thinking mind, the sensitive heart: what can I do? How can I make a difference?

The answer is clear: we must make a start; we must make a difference, in our own, small, humble way. We must learn to live at peace with ourselves. We must learn to live in harmony with Mother Nature and God's Universe. We must learn to live and let live. We must feel at one with all of God's creation. We must recognise and respect the inviolate sanctity of all life! We do not require manpower, materials, resources and backup to do this: all it takes is a little sensitivity, a little compassion, a little self-discipline and commitment to the values of *ahimsa*. And we will be amazed at the difference it makes to our lives and attitudes. The change that we seek can begin with as simple a thing as our diet.

Man cannot live without air, water and food. While air and water are available to us in the natural state, food is selected, prepared and eaten by our own choice. My appeal to you through the pages of this book is: make the right choice for your food practices!

In practical terms food can be of two categories: food of violence or *himsa*– food that includes fish, flesh and fowl; the alternative is the food of *ahimsa* or non-violence – in other words, a vegetarian diet. During the last fifty years or more, medical experts and nutritionists have largely inclined to the opinion that a vegetarian diet is the best option for good health. This book is a humble effort to promote that option.

It is my firm belief that the food of non-violence is the diet of the new age; vegetarianism is the way of life for the Twenty First Century – indeed, for the new millennium. Vegetarianism is no longer the diet of the neglected few, the freak or the eccentric.

People all over the world are turning to a vegetarian diet, for it has been recognised as a way of life which promotes health and the ancient *rishi* of the Ishopanishad sang, *Ishavasyam Idam Sarvam*: all that is, is a vesture of the Lord. God comes to us, putting on different vestures, different garments. Clad in different garbs, the Lord comes to us to test us, to find out if we truly love Him, as we say we do.

Alas! We slay the Lord! We handle Him roughly, we treat Him harshly! We offer Him worship in temples and churches; we chant hymns to His glory – but out in the street we are cruel to Him!

We slay Him and eat His flesh! We forget that the animal too, is an image of God! The Tamil Saint Thiruvalluvar asks us: "How can he be possessed of kindness, who, to increase his own flesh, eats the flesh of other creatures?"

Are you aware, that on an average, a person eats 7500 animals in a lifetime? The time has come when we must decide once and for all, that all types of exploitation, all types of human tyranny must cease, if we are to have lasting peace in the world. It is only through a shared reverence for all life that the dream of world peace can be turned into a realisable goal. Every animal has some fundamental rights – and the time has come when we must formulate a charter of animal rights. This naturally implies a charter of man's duties towards the animal kingdom. The very first fundamental right of an animal is the right to live. No man can take away that which he cannot give. Since we cannot give life to a dead creature, it goes without saying that we have no right to take away the life of a living one, just to pamper our palates and indulge our taste buds.

Let us therefore, cultivate what Gurudev Sadhu Vaswani calls "Cosmic Consciousness" – to commune with the earth-spirit, to have a new feeling for the 'animal' world. For the so-called 'lower' animals are also children of Mother Earth. To treat them harshly is wrong. To take them to the slaughterhouse is a sin.

This then, is the purpose of this book on vegetarianism – not to preach, but to help you practice a way of life which is bound to be your first step towards a more sensitive, caring, compassionate, healthful way of life.

And what better way to end this dedication than by echoing the words of Gurudev Sadhu Vaswani: "Yes! These animals are your brothers! Kill them not! Believe me, meat eating will one day be condemned as murder!"

– J. P. Vaswani

Contents

CHAPTER ONE

WHAT IS VEGETARIANISM?

Naivedya:

Then God said, "I give you every seed-bearing plant on the face of the whole earth and every tree that has fruit with seed in it. They will be yours for food."

— Genesis 1:29

———◆———

Invocation:

I have seen God's image shinning in birds and animals and for me not to love birds and animals, would be not to love the Lord.

— Sadhu Vaswani

———◆———

Apertif:

Vegetarian food leaves a deep impression on our nature. If the whole world adopts vegetarianism, it can change the destiny of humankind.

— Albert Einstein

———◆———

✦ Starters ✦

The local church in a Mid Western American town was planning a banquet for its members and everyone was urged to attend. There was a cost involved for each couple and one vegetarian couple in the church decided not to attend because the menu was a prefixed one and did not fit with their meatless lifestyle. However, the organisers of the dinner assured them that a vegetarian meal could be provided and so they signed up and paid their fee. At the banquet, the meal began with a green salad in a small wooden salad bowl.

When the time came for the entrée, after serving everyone else, the waitress brought the two vegetarians each a very large salad, identical to the one they had just eaten, in a very large wooden salad bowl—the size that would normally contain all of the salad for a family of four! In other words, first there was salad as an appetiser, and then there was SALAD as the entrée! Apparently, the chef's imagination as to what vegetarians eat did not go beyond a green salad!

✦ Main Course ✦

Vegetarianism is perhaps one of the most misunderstood concepts of our times. "Grass eaters", "salad eaters", freaks, eccentrics, cranks and herbivores are some of the terms used with equal parts of derision and affection to refer to vegetarians. Quite apart from such attitudinal descriptions, misconceptions and prejudices are also attached to this much maligned dietary system.

Twenty or thirty years ago, it might have been difficult for us to find unbiased, systematic, comprehensive information on vegetarianism in the form of a book or a website. This was a time when vegetarianism was regarded as "the cult of the crazy". It was also the butt of several ill-informed jokes. Let me share a few with you:

A man suffered from chronic insomnia or sleeplessness. His doctor advised him to induce sleep by counting sheep.

The man protested, "But I can't! I am a vegetarian."

The doctor said, "In that case, count carrots."

Happily, such rampant prejudice is no longer the norm today. In fact, we can say that the tide is turning. Apart from those who are born to a vegetarian lifestyle, several thousands of people in East and West are turning to vegetarianism as a lifestyle that promotes health and well-being.

Though I am not a great believer or creator of

definitions, I must admit I am deeply interested in etymology and word origins. The Latin root *vegere is* thought of as the source of the term vegetarianism: *vegere means* 'active'; related words in this group are 'vigil', 'vigour' and 'awake'. Enthusiastic vegetarians also trace the roots of their chosen diet system to the Latin word *vegetus,* meaning "whole, sound, fresh and lively". It is said that the Vegetarian Society created the word vegetarian from the Latin *vegetus* meaning 'lively' (which is how these early vegetarians claimed their diet made them feel) in 1847, and that is how the term gained currency in the West. The records of the Vegetarian Society tell us that "the term ... was first formally used on September 30th of that year by Joseph Brotherton and others, at Northwood Villa in Kent, England. The occasion being the inaugural meeting of the Vegetarian Society of the United Kingdom..." Vegetarian enthusiasts with a sense of humour note rather gleefully that the American vegetarian movement was initiated by two people named Cowherd and Metcalfe. It is presumed that their surnames engendered their sensitivity to the consumption of cows and calfs and other four-legged friends!

We are told too, that prior to 1847, non-meat eaters were generally known as "Pythagoreans" or adherents of the "Pythagorean System", after the ancient Greek "vegetarian" Pythagoras.

An interesting earlier use of the term is attributed

to a gentleman in America, a plantation owner, who wrote in his journal in 1839: "If I had to be my own cook, I should inevitably become a vegetarian."

Yet others who think that this derivation is rather self-aggrandising, frown at what they regard as self-promotion of vegetarianism and insist that the term is formed simply from the word *vegetable* and the suffix *-arian* (like the one found in agrarian, librarian, etc.).

The word vegetarianism is mostly used to refer to the commonly accepted meaning: that is, a dietary practice that avoids the use of flesh foods. However, I must make a distinction between one whom I love to think of as a 'true vegetarian' and others whose vegetarianism stops with their diet.

What are the marks of a 'true vegetarian'?

The true vegetarian, as I think of him, is filled through and through with reverence for life. He reveres life as a gift of God which no man can bestow and, therefore, will not destroy. Such a one has the following marks:

1) His heart is a flowing river of compassion and love. The basis of true compassion is a feeling of unity, of oneness with all creatures that breathe the breath of life. I, and that tiny winged creature that hovers around a lamp, are one. Men and animals and birds, fish and fowl, moths and

mosquitoes – all, all are one in the One without whom there is no other. To the true vegetarian, therefore, each life-unit is as dear and precious as his own life. To him every dumb creature of God is his own self wearing another body. And so the true vegetarian will not be a party to any movement for slaughter. On his banner are inscribed the words in letters of fire: *Stop all slaughter!*

2) The true vegetarian is a man of self-discipline. So many there are who do not eat flesh but, alas, they easily succumb to the flesh. They cannot resist the temptations of the flesh. They are soft: they have not put out the fire of passion. The true vegetarian is unswayed by passion, unruffled by anger, unmoved by greed and gold.

3) The true vegetarian is a man of humility. Deep in his heart he knows that he is not free from the sin of killing. For to breathe is to kill the germs that are in the air around us. To talk is to kill; to walk is to kill. Indeed, to live is to kill.

4) Living in such a world, the true vegetarian becomes a worshipper, a man of prayer. He sees cruelty all around him. How many hearts can he touch? How many lives can he save? And so he turns to Him who is the one Saviour of all. The true vegetarian prays alike for the killer and the killed and he prays that he may become an instrument of God's love in this world of anguish

and pain.

5) The true vegetarian is a man of indomitable faith. He believes profoundly that life is entirely a gift of God. In periods of crisis, in times of famine and flood, his mind wavers not! He prefers starvation to eating impure food. To the Sufi *dervish*, Abu Ala Maeera, his physician said, "O man of God! Why will you not live longer and bless this earth? Drink this chicken soup I have brought for you and see how quickly health and strength returns to your feeble body." The *dervish* laughed heartily and said, "Must you offer me the soup of a weak, defenseless creature who cannot strike back in return? Is it not worthy of you! Bring me the soup of a lion's cub!"

✦ *Food for Thought* ✦

According to United Nations sources, more than half of the world's people are hungry or malnourished, and nearly half of them have barely enough food on which to survive.

Are we using our land in the most practical and productive manner?

It has been found that arable land will support far more human beings per acre, if devoted to the growing of vegetable matter for direct human consumption, than for raising animals for food.

According to Isaac Asimov, noted biochemist and professor at the Boston University School of Medicine, "At each step of feeding there is considerable waste so that only 10 percent of the living matter of the creature fed upon is converted into the living matter of the creature who is feeding." Taking the ecological chain one link further, he says that a creature living on other carnivorous creatures would only return about 1% (10% of 10%) of the food value eaten by the first creatures in the chain. On the other hand, "By cutting out items in the food chain, then, a feeder can do better in terms of its own numbers and mass". He makes the point that if we were to bypass just one link in the ecological food-chain, we "would then have a food supply ten times as great" compared with the former, second-hand food source. (*Where Do We Go From Here?* — Fawcett Crest Book, edited by Dr.

Asimov, 10/72 ed., page 247.)

Slightly more than half of the acreage harvested in the United States is planted with crops for animal-feed: 91% of the corn, 77% of the soybean meal, 64% of the barley, and 88% of the oat cropis fed to animals instead of to people. If these tremendous food resources were rechanneled for direct human consumption, our present food shortage would cease to exist, and would instead become a whopping surplus.

www.highvibrations.org

Dessert

The standard diet of a meat-eater is blood, flesh, veins, muscles, tendons, cow secretions, hen periods and bee vomit. And once a year during a certain holiday in November, meat-eaters use the hollowed-out hind regions of a dead bird as a pressure cooker for stuffing. And people think vegans are weird because we eat tofu?

- Vegan bodybuilder Robert Cheeke

CHAPTER TWO

WHY WE SHOULD SAY NO TO MEAT

Naivedya:

There is no beast on earth, no bird which flieth but... the same is a people like unto you. All God's creatures are God's family.

– The Holy Quran

Invocation:

Man is the elder brother of the animal. So must man be the animal's guardian and helper, not his tyrant and oppressor.

– Sadhu Vaswani

Apertif:

Vegetables are primary sources nourished by the sun and soil while meat is a secondary source nourished and sustained by vegetables.

– Dr. Christopher Gian Cuisio
Nutritionist

✦ Starters ✦

It is a common myth that Adolf Hitler, the most infamous Nazi dictator of the 20th century, was a vegetarian. No doubt, it would be supremely ironic if he were, especially to those engaged in the fierce propaganda war against vegetarianism. But research has proved that this is just another anti-vegetarian myth.

Biographers like Albert Speer, Robert Payne, John Toland, have all attested to Hitler's fondness for sausages, among other things, and Hitler's personal cook, Dione Lucas, reported that Hitler was particularly fond of stuffed pigeon. However, from the 1930s, Hitler was constrained to give up meat quite often, even if it was only temporarily, to counter his growing bouts of abdominal pain, flatulence and excessive sweatiness. But he never lost his lifelong fondness for game birds or caviar.

These dietary experiments, coupled with Joseph Goebbels' propagandistic image of Hitler as some sort of pure ascetic, no doubt contributed to the propagation of the myth that Hitler was a vegetarian.

✦ Main Course ✦

We live in an age when eating non-vegetarian food is considered to be the ultimate gastronomic delight; many misguided youngsters think that red meat, fish and chicken are trendy, exotic and energising. "How can we live without meat?" is the cry heard from many youngsters, even those born into vegetarian families.

In this *kaliyug*, pampering the palate has become everyone's supreme indulgence. We live to eat rather than eat to live. No one who delights in non-vegetarian food is ready to accept that their choice of diet entails a lot of cruelty to our animal brethren.

Many people continue to believe that God created animals to provide food for man. If this is indeed so, why should animals scream and howl in pain when they are slaughtered? Perhaps you will argue that they have not read the scriptures!

A holy man I know tells his disciples who still want to eat meat, "Fine! But don't buy the meat. Kill the animal yourself, and eat him." Many of us continue to eat flesh only because someone else does all the killing and the bloodshed, and the meat is brought, beautifully prepared to our table!

In an interesting book which I read years ago, Dr. Edwin Flatto argues that those who eat flesh food are only eating grains and vegetables second hand. The animals which they eat – cows, goats, sheep, chicken, etc – receive their nutrition from vegetables and grains. These animals pass on the nutrition they have received to the meat-eaters. How much better it would be if they got it directly!

The famous vegetarian, Dr. Kellogg says, "When we eat vegetarian food, we don't have to worry about what kind of disease the food died of. That makes a joyful meal!"

If there is one thing that people have come to fear as much as a nuclear explosion, it is that dreaded substance called cholesterol. Increased level of cholesterol in the blood is responsible for coronary heart disease and also gall-stones. It is now a well-known fact that animal fats raise the cholesterol level in the blood. Further, the saturated fatty acids in animal fat aggravate coronary heart disease.

Cholesterol is actually a steroid present in all animal cells. It occurs in almost all foods of animal origin, such as meat, fish, milk, cream, cheese, eggs and butter. Cholesterol is present in the fat portion of these foods. Most foods of plant origin – such as fruits, vegetables, cereals – do not contain cholesterol.

Research has proved that animal fats raise the cholesterol level of the blood, while certain vegetables actually lower it.

Another factor we must consider in evaluating the health aspects of a non-vegetarian diet is this: that the amount of toxic wastes present in the flesh of a dead animal are very high. Thus, when we eat the flesh of animals, we are not only consuming the so-called nutritive portions, but also these poisonous waste-products. It is not possible for the body to eliminate these poisons immediately and effectively.

These are largely 'scientific' reasons for not eating meat: these and other factors will be discussed under the ethical, philosophical, medical, aesthetic and economic reasons for choosing a vegetarian diet. What I want to stress in this section is my dearly held belief that man has a mystic sense of kinship with all creation, all that lives; this is what makes every life sacred; this is why, in my thinking, meat-eating must be condemned as murder of non-human creatures!

Gurudev Sadhu Vaswani was a voice of the voiceless ones, those dumb, defenceless children of God who, alas, are being slain by the million in our soulless cities everyday! "O, the sin of daily slaughter!" he exclaimed, adding words with which many people today will not be in sympathy. But those words were spoken with the foresight of a seer and a prophet, when he said, "Believe me, the day is coming when meat-eating will be condemned as murder!"

Gurudev was the very embodiment of compassion. He said, "I have seen God's image shining in birds and animals, and for me not to love bird and animal would be not to love the Lord!"

So profound were the effect of his words that many of us embraced the ideal of vegetarianism and animal rights, and felt the need to raise our voices, to stand up and be counted against the cruelties that are perpetrated on animals and birds day after day. When a delicious dish of flesh or fowl is placed before a man, he eats it as a matter of right, a matter of routine. He does not, for a moment realise the implications of his choice; he does not even so much as spare a thought for the agony through which the slaughtered animal must have passed!

Whenever I say this, people retort: "Why should I concern myself with the suffering of animals when there are so many people suffering in the world today?"

It is true that many people are suffering: they too, deserve our care and compassion! All life is sacred: we need reverence for all; those above us, those around us, those below us. Essentially the tendency to hurt another, the tendency to be indifferent to another's suffering has to be plucked out of our minds and hearts completely.

Then the river of compassion will flow and benefit humanity at large – both men and animals.

When you are awakened to the fact that all life is One; all life is sacred; when you have a universalist view of life, you will be filled with love and compassion for all beings. Human suffering is greater than animal suffering; but animals have no voice, they cannot communicate their suffering, they look up to human beings for kindness and comfort. Man can protect himself; his friends and fellow humans will come to his aid; he can call a doctor, hire the ambulance, fight for his survival... Is it not incumbent upon man, with his superior sixth sense, to protect his dumb and defenseless brethren?

Do you know how animals are tortured before they are slaughtered? I suggest that you watch the video clip titled, "Meet Your Meat" which is widely available on the Internet. Let me warn you: It is horrifying! Just to get the momentary pleasure of taste, just to indulge the palate, people turn a blind eye to the cruel slaughter of innocent creatures day after day, and only focus on devouring their flesh.

Even though they are aware that meat-eating has been proved to be injurious to health, they become slaves to the tongue!

I believe that he who kills another, kills his own spirit! He who feeds on death, himself becomes food for death. He who inflicts suffering upon another, brings suffering upon himself. Such is the law.

Every bit of flesh you tear, you will be called upon to repair with your own flesh! Every limb you mutilate, you will be compelled to replace with your own limb! And every bone you break, or cause to be broken for your need, you will be asked to mend with your own bone!

Animal welfare is not enough! We must speak of animal rights!

Men have their rights; have animals no rights? I believe the time has come when all animal lovers must get together and formulate a charter of animal rights— a charter of man's duties towards the animal kingdom. I hope and pray that India—the country of the Buddha, Mahavira, Mahatma Gandhi and Sadhu Vaswani—will be among the first nations to pass an enactment giving rights which are due to animals.

Every animal has some fundamental rights. And the very first right of every animal is the right to live! We cannot take away that which we cannot give! And since we cannot give life to a dead creature, we have no right to take away the life of a living one! The time is come, when we must decide once and for all, that all types of human exploitation and tyranny must cease. We must recognise the moral inviolability of individual rights—both human and nonhuman.

Just as black people don't exist as resources for white people, just as the poor don't exist as resources for the rich, just as women don't exist as resources for men, even so animals don't exist as resources for human beings! In the words of Gurudev Sadhu Vaswani, "No nation can be free, until its animals are free!" The world cannot be at peace until all forms of exploitation cease!

✦ *Food for Thought* ✦

The human digestive system, tooth and jaw structure, and bodily functions are completely different from carnivorous animals.

As in the case of the anthropoid ape, the human digestive system is twelve times the length of the body; our skin has millions of tiny pores to evaporate water and cool the body by sweating; we drink water by suction like all other vegetarian animals; our tooth and jaw structure is vegetarian; and our saliva is alkaline and contains ptyalin for predigestion of grains. Human beings clearly are not carnivores by physiology our anatomy and digestive system show that we must have evolved for millions of years living on fruits, nuts, grains, and vegetables.

Furthermore, it is obvious that our natural instincts are non-carnivorous. Most people have other people kill their meat for them and would be sickened if they had to do the killing themselves.

Instead of eating raw meat as all flesh-eating animals do, humans boil, bake, or fry it and disguise it with all kinds of sauces and spices so that it bears no resemblance to its raw state. One scientist explains it this way: "A cat will salivate with hungry desire at the smell of a piece of raw flesh but not at all at the smell of fruit.

If man could delight in pouncing upon a bird, tear its still-living limbs apart with his teeth, and suck the warm blood, one might conclude that nature provided him with meat-eating instinct. On the other hand, a bunch of luscious grapes makes his mouth water, and even in the absence of hunger he will eat fruit because it tastes so good."

Scientists and naturalists, including the great Charles Darwin who gave the theory of evolution, agree that early humans were fruit and vegetable eaters and that throughout history our anatomy has not changed. The great Swedish scientist von Linnaeus states:

"Man's structure, external and internal, compared with that of the other animals, shows that fruit and succulent vegetables constitute his natural food."

www.bnvillage.co.uk

Dessert

Albert Schweitzer's ethical system was encapsulated by his call for reverence for life. One day, while showing a visitor around his hospital in Lambarene (in Gabon, Africa), he happened to see a dog eagerly chasing a frantic chicken in the yard. "No! No!" Schweitzer cried. "Remember we have won the Nobel Peace Prize!"

CHAPTER THREE

THE CONCEPT OF NON-VIOLENCE

Naivedya:

Ahimsa is the highest *dharma*. *Ahimsa* is the best *tapas*. *Ahimsa* is the greatest gift. *Ahimsa* is the highest self-control. *Ahimsa* is the noblest sacrifice. *Ahimsa* is the highest power. *Ahimsa* is the best friend. *Ahimsa* is the highest truth. *Ahimsa* is the highest teaching.

— Mahabharata XVIII:116.37-41.

Invocation:

To live in *Ahimsa* is to live in sweetness and light. *Ahimsa* is peace with all. *Ahimsa* is harmony. *Ahimsa* is attunnement to the Life Universal. *Ahimsa* is self-surrender to the One Life, the One Spirit, the One Divine Will that works in all.

— Sadhu Vaswani

Apertif:

My religion is based on truth and non-violence. Truth is my God. Non-violence is the means of realising Him.

— Mahatma Gandhi

✦ Starters ✦

Aikido is a Japanese martial art based upon the same principle as *Ahimsa*. It teaches mental and physical techniques that allow the practitioner to meet aggression with compassion, not fear, and to use soft strength to redirect negative energy so that no harm befalls either person. It is said that the physical techniques of Aikido do not work until one masters compassion, and once this is done, the physical techniques are no longer necessary.

An American was living in Japan and studying Aikido. One day, while he was riding on a train, a very powerful (and very drunk) labourer climbed into the carriage. As the American watched, the labourer started pushing people around, finally knocking over a woman carrying a child.

Knowing that someone needed to do something, and seeing that no one else was going to stand up to the man, the American realised that at last he was going to get an opportunity to find out whether his years of intensive Aikido training had prepared him for conflict in the real world. The American stood, attracting the attention of the drunken worker, who locked eyes with him. Because Aikido techniques only work in response to attack, the American provoked the drunk, by blowing him a kiss. With a bellow, the man lumbered down the carriage, picking up speed as he came.

Remaining calm, the American relaxed his body as he had been trained, dropped his centre of gravity, and prepared to meet the rush of his attacker.

Just then the carriage rang out with a sharp yet strangely joyful "HEY!!!" that made the worker stop short in his tracks. Wheeling to confront his new antagonist, the drunk saw a little old man who sat there smiling at him; he was shocked at being challenged by such a frail creature. "What have you been drinking?" asked the old man with a mischievous grin. Taken aback, the worker replied, "Sake."

The old man, nodded. Still smiling, he said "Sake is good, is it not?" Confused, the worker nodded in agreement. The old man continued, "My wife and I like to drink Sake together. Every evening we like to sit in our garden and drink Sake while we watch the sunset and admire the beautiful persimmon tree that my great-grandfather planted. Every year the persimmon tree grows larger and stronger. It is so wonderful to share such simple pleasures with my wife." He looked at the worker, questioningly, "Do you have a wife?" The labourer dropped his head and replied haltingly, "My wife died... I got no wife... I got no home... I got no job. I am so ashamed of myself."

As the train pulled into the next station, the American watched the labourer, seated beside the old man, sobbing, with his head buried in the old man's lap. As he left the train he saw the old man stroke the labourer's head and heard him whisper that it would be all right. The American realised that, for all of his training, he had a lot to learn about practising Aikido in the real world.

✦ Main Course ✦

It was in a pensive mood that Mahatma Gandhi penned these words in 1946:

Perhaps never before has there been so much speculation about the future as there is today. Will our world always be one of violence? Will there always be poverty, starvation, misery? Will we have a firmer and wide belief in religion, or will the world be Godless? If there is to be a great change in society, how will that change be wrought? By war, or revolution? Or will it come peacefully?

Different men give different answers to these questions, each man drawing the plan of tomorrow's world as he hopes and wishes it to be. I answer not only out of belief but out of conviction. The world of tomorrow will be, must be, a society based on non-violence. That is the first law; out of it all other blessings will flow. It may seem a distant goal, an impractical Utopia. But it is not in the least unobtainable, since it can be worked for here and now. An individual can adopt the way of life of the future – the non-violent way, without having to wait for others to do so. And if an individual can do it, cannot whole groups of individuals? Whole nations? Men often hesitate to make a beginning because they feel that the objective cannot be achieved in its entirety. This attitude of mind is precisely our greatest obstacle to progress – an obstacle that each man, if he only wills it, can clear away.

In an age which believes that war and violence can be justified as 'means' to achieve desirable ends, Gandhiji's emphasis on non-violence may seem obsolete and impractical: but the Hindu way of life has always taught us that *ahimsa* is the greatest virtue: *ahimsa paramo dharma.*

Sri Swami Sivananda rightly observes that *ahimsa* is a subtle and profound ideal which is not just limited to non-killing. In its comprehensive meaning, *ahimsa* or non-injury means complete abstinence from causing any pain or harm whatsoever to any living creature, either by thought, word, or deed. Non-injury is not an abstract philosophy; at its most basic, it requires us to think harmless thoughts, utter non-injurious words as well as perform non-violent deeds.

Therefore, *ahimsa* is not just an act of omission, but a form of positive, cosmic love. Contempt for others, dislike and prejudice towards people, speaking ill of others, gossip, slander, use of harsh language to inferiors, rude speech, uttering lies, discourtesy, unkindness, and failure to help others and relieve others' distress are all different forms of non-violence. Hurting the feelings or sentiments of others is also a form of injury. Cursing, swearing and harsh criticism are all aspects of *ahimsa*. Even harsh gestures, angry looks and an aggressive tone of voice are acts of *himsa or violence*. Little wonder then, that *ahimsa* takes us close to the Divine within each one of us.

Nor should we regard *ahimsa* as a passive attitude, as the resort of the weak and the powerless: on the other hand, it is a dynamic, positive force which is achieved only by those who are spiritually strong. For those of you who wish to cultivate this great virtue, my advice would be to begin with the *tapasya* of the tongue: do not utter harsh, angry and foul words; control your speech; then, at the next level, control your palate: do not crave for foods of violence.

If you practise this for a few days, you will find that violent and cruel thoughts gradually begin to leave your mind and heart. Not finding a physical outlet through speech, thoughts of cruelty, anger and revenge die out gradually, and are replaced by calm and peaceful thoughts.

Jesus Christ said to his disciples: "You have heard that the ancients were told, You shall not commit murder and Whoever commits murder shall be liable to the court. But, I say to you that everyone who is angry with his brother shall be guilty before the court; and whoever says to his brother, 'You good-for-nothing', shall be guilty before the supreme court; and whoever says, 'You fool', shall be guilty enough to go into the fiery hell." In its essence, this is non-violence in words! Notice too that Jesus does not stop with acts of omission like do-not-commit-murder; he goes one step further in fact, many steps further and tells us:

You have heard that it was said, "An eye for an eye, and

a tooth for a tooth." But I say to you, do not resist an evil person; but whoever slaps you on your right cheek, turn the other to him also. If anyone wants to sue you and take your shirt, let him have your coat also.

Whoever forces you to go one mile, go with him two. Give to him who asks of you, and do not turn away from him who wants to borrow from you.

You have heard that it was said, "You shall love your neighbour and hate your enemy."

But I say to you, love your enemies and pray for those who persecute you, so that you may be sons of your Father who is in heaven; for He causes His sun to rise on the evil and the good, and sends rain on the righteous and the unrighteous. For if you love those who love you, what reward do you have? Do not even the tax collectors do the same? If you greet only your brothers, what more are you doing than others? Do not even the Gentiles do the same? Therefore you are to be perfect, as your heavenly Father is perfect.

In a sense, the Sermon on the Mount sets out the highest ideals of non-violence in thought, word and attitude. Do you know that many Christians believe that these were not actually meant to be practised? Even great thinkers like St. Augustine and Thomas Aquinas felt that the ideals were meant for perception, but the injunctions were to be obeyed only by monks and clergy; Martin Luther divided the world into the religious and secular realms and argued that the Sermon only applied to the spiritual. In the temporal world, obligations to family, employers, and country force believers to compromise. Thus, a judge should follow his secular obligations to sentence a criminal, but inwardly, he should mourn for the fate of the criminal.

I mention this only to show to you that non-violence is the highest ideal and closest to Divinity; so much so that in daily life we tend to water it down, dilute it or re-interpret it to suit our convenience! Thus some early copyists changed Matthew 5:22 from "whosoever is angry with his brother shall be in danger of the judgement" to the watered-down "whosoever is angry with his brother *without a cause* shall be in danger of the judgement." And again, "Love your enemies" was changed conveniently to "Love one another".

No, *ahimsa* is not easy to practise in its true and pure form! But even attempting the impossible can bring us countless blessings and benefits. As our ancient *rishis* tell us, *ahimsa* is the pivot around which all virtues revolve. It is the soul-force that enables us to attain all virtues. It purifies our hearts and minds; it gives us strong willpower and self-discipline; it enhances our spiritual strength; ultimately it enables us to realise God and enter the realm of the Blessed.

A final word on the subject of *ahimsa* towards non-human creatures: for we have been so concerned with the difficulties of practising non-violence in daily life towards other people, that we are often apt to overlook the fact that this principle should also extend to all living things and beings: this is why *ahimsa* is a favourite ideal with environmentalists all over the world. The degradation of the forests, the raids on natural resources, the failure to protect endangered species, the cruel slaughter of animals and poultry for human consumption – these are also forms of *himsa* that we practise on the world of creation around us. True *ahimsa* is a binding code of conduct that requires us to be sensitive to the pain of non-human creatures. Cruelty to these creatures brings with it the danger of negative *karmic* consequences, according to the Hindu tradition.

Animals and plants also have physical sensations; they too experience pain and pleasure, although we may not be aware of it. They also have their own form of life and sensation although it may not be highly developed or sophisticated. Thus, all living beings deserve our consideration and kindness. Even as we try to avoid personal pain and suffering, even as we desist from causing pain and suffering to other humans, so should we deal with the rest of creation. Interfering with other life-forms is also *ahimsa* – a violation of the sanctity of life.

✦ *Food for Thought* ✦

In times of military duty, Baha'i ask for a special category, that of "non-combatant". In times of national emergency, this moral stance allows them to serve as stretcher-bearers, ambulance corps, office administrators, relief workers and so forth. In so doing, Baha'i do not seek a safe berth from combat in times of national crisis. Driving an ambulance can be a very risky form of service.

A Baha'i may also enlist voluntarily in the armed forces to make a career, or to learn a trade or profession, provided that he or she can do so without being liable to undertake combatant service – i.e. engaging in actual warfare or killing others.

– Jack Maclean, Baha'i scholar

Dessert

Pay more for milk and eggs to help the animals retire happy. SHOPPERS are being invited to pay £2.45 a litre for milk and £2.99, or 50p each, for six eggs, in order to fund long life and retirement for the cows and hens. The prices are being charged in Selfridges in London for products from vegetarian entrepreneur and fashion designer, Isobel Davies.

The idea for her *Cow Nation* and *Hen Nation* ventures grew out of charging enough for her clothes to pay for natural life spans for the 600 Wensleydale sheep which provide wool for her fashion store at Richmond.

She and a sympathiser, Liz Jones, author of Liz Jones's Diary, bought a mixed bag of 60 cows of all ages, mainly Jerseys, from a struggling dairy farmer in Suffolk, and hired him to keep the cows as long as they could keep going without suffering. Then they found an organic eggs producer in Surrey willing to run a flock of 1,680 laying hens on the same basis.

A small business called Ahimsa Milk already delivers milk in the London area from a farm run on Buddhist principles in Kent and charges £2.40 a litre for doorstep delivery.

Courtesy: *Yorkshire Post*

CHAPTER FOUR

THE INVIOLABLE
SANCTITY OF LIFE

Naivedya:

Do not injure the beings living on the earth, in the air and in the water.

– Yajur Veda

Invocation:

Holy, holy, holy is every creature!
Touch ye these children of the Lord with reverence and love!
Harm them not! But serve them in deep humility!

– Sadhu Vaswani

Apertif:

By *ahimsa* Patanjali meant the removal of the desire to kill. All forms of life have an equal right to the air of *maya*. The saint who uncovers the secret of creation will be in harmony with Nature's countless bewildering expressions. All men may understand this truth by overcoming the passion for destruction.

– Sri Yukteswar to Paramahansa Yogananda

✦ Starters ✦

The Vietnam War featured the most intense bombing campaign in military history. Between March 1965 and November 1968, Operation "Rolling Thunder" deluged the north of Vietnam with a million tons of missiles, rockets and bombs. The bomb tonnage dropped during the Vietnam War amounted to 1,000 lbs. for every man, woman and child in Vietnam. An estimated 3 million people were killed by the war, and over 1 million were wounded.

The US introduced the use of defoliants, most famously napalm, a form of jellied gasoline. One bomber group's slogan was: "Only you can prevent forests". During the war about 1/2 of Vietnam's rain forests were destroyed. The soldiers were indoctrinated to believe that somehow, the Vietnamese were less than human, and that killing them by such infamous means was legitimate in American interests.

The military top brass failed to anticipate the psychological impact of the bombing on American pilots, who flew their helicopters above the dense forests and lush paddy fields, and could not often see the target of their carpet bombing. But this proved to be disastrous for the pilots. After the war, the psychological burdens the men carried during the war continued to haunt them. Those who survived the war carried guilt, grief, and confusion, and many of them failed to come to terms with their experience.

✦ Main Course ✦

The phrase 'sanctity of life' embraces concepts of religion, ethics, morality and law. It is based on the idea that all life is sacred, and the right to life of every creature is inviolable. This also implies that all life is to be protected and all attempts to violate or endanger the life of any sentient creature amount to a violation of the sanctity of God's creation. In western philosophy, this principle is applied to human lives alone, for it is only human beings who are said to be created 'in God's image' with an immortal soul. Thus Sanctity of Life proponents in the U.S. for example, are concerned largely with issues like abortion, euthanasia and war crimes. But in Indian thought and philosophy, the sanctity of life principle extends to all forms of creation, for all forms of life, human, animal, plant and mineral are thought of as embodiments of the One transcendental Life force that permeates the entire Universe.

Of course man is the crown of creation, the undisputed sovereign of planet Earth. Of course human rights is a worthy cause, and human life is precious. But the stand taken by animal rights activists and humble advocates of the ideal of Reverence for All Life like myself is this: we object to the arbitrary discrimination that non-human lives are expendable and can be freely sacrificed to satisfy the human palate;

we think it morally and ethically wrong to inflict needless pain and suffering on dumb and defenceless creatures just because they do not belong to our human species! Our understanding of the sanctity of life teaches us that oppression and exploitation must end wherever they are allowed to occur.

In the year 1975, Peter Singer published his path-breaking book, *Animal Liberation*. Shortly before the launch, he was invited by several animal lovers to share their concerns and issues. Many of them wanted to know about his pets, and were scandalised to hear that he did not have any. In their dictionary, animal lover meant someone who owned cute animals like poodles and kittens and gerbils, stroked furry creatures and fed birds in the garden. They were quite baffled that he was not a lover of cute animals, but someone who was appalled by the way flesh food was produced for human consumption in factory farms. Their love for animals was soft and sentimental; but he was horrified by roast beef, ham sandwiches, fried chickens and all other forms of dead animals that were brought to the family dining table as favourite foods.

They were ready to raise their voices for dogs and horses; he was equally concerned about pigs and chickens. Their love for their pets verged on emotion and sentimentality; he was fighting to apply uniform moral standards to the pain and suffering inflicted on human and non-human animals! Their love for animals did not extend to the least sensitivity for creatures slaughtered ruthlessly in mechanised factories; his idea of the sanctity of life made him extend the principle of equality to all creatures, human and non-human. They understood the discriminatory practices of racists and sexists who opposed the rights of blacks and women; he was concerned about *speceisists* – human beings who refused to recognise the rights of animals!

Speciesists, according to Singer, are insensitive people, bigots who claim that animals have no rights, no interests and therefore deserve no special defence. They assume most gratuitously, that animals feel no pain and they cannot suffer. They would protest loudly against killing human beings; but they are only too willing to permit the killing of animals for human consumption. For them, only human life is sacrosanct; other creatures' lives are expendable.

In the Twentieth Century, people's attitude to animals definitely changed for the better; many activists began fighting to protect wild life and endangered species; they are advocating better living conditions and ethical treatment of animals in the circus and the zoo. But these very activists are silent on the issue of exploiting animals and killing them for human consumption! Even societies which work for the prevention of cruelty to animals restrict their activities to caring for stray dogs and prosecuting acts of wanton cruelty towards animals. They leave factory farms and slaughter houses well alone.

Human beings claim that they are far superior to animals; but when it comes to food, they point out that animals are carnivorous and often kill other animals for food, using this as a justification of killing animals for meat! These people refer to the 'savagery' and the 'bestial nature' of wild animals, and use terms such as 'brutal' and 'savage' to refer to low and base natures; they themselves are, in contrast, 'humane' and 'compassionate' and 'sensitive'! But it is, in reality, we the people who kill for the least reason. We call lions and wolves savage because they kill smaller animals and tear into their flesh. But we kill animals for 'fun' and 'sport' when we hunt; we kill rare species and strip them of their fur to beautify our costumes; we permit the torture and slaughter of harmless animals to tickle our palate. And, of course, some of us do not stop at killing other beings of our own species for selfish ends like power, profit or revenge. I fail to see how we are superior to savage animals, and why we should consider our own lives more sacrosanct than the lives of other creatures!

To get back to my starting point, I repeat the *vedantic* doctrine that the One life manifests itself in all creation: it sleeps in the stone, it dreams in the plants, it stirs in animals and it wakes in man. These stages also serve to indicate that animals are capable of feeling pain and suffering, while plants are not. There are many people who object loudly: "How do you know that plants do not feel pain and do not suffer when you pluck their fruits for food?"

If this question is raised out of genuine concern for plant life, I welcome this concern heartily. But their interest is only to justify killing animals for food, on the ground that a vegetarian diet too destroys plant life, and therefore cannot be a moral or ethical alternative to flesh food. Therefore, they conclude, what difference does it make whether we eat animals or plants? We have got to eat in order to live; we might as well eat plants and/or animals.

Plants do not have a central nervous system as animals do; there is no observable 'behaviour' that suggests to us that they suffer; their evolutionary status is such that they are stationary, and cannot move or run, and therefore, incapable of feeling pain. In short, "Plants feel pain" is only a specious, devious argument used to discredit vegetarians, and not really an answer to the protests against cruelty to animals.

My final argument is one which I have stated again and again: we do not have the right to take away that which we cannot give back. I can take away the life of an animal: but I cannot give it back to the animal I have killed. The life of that animal is as precious, as dear to the creature as my life is to me. Therefore, I have no right to take the life of an animal for any reason – scientific, experimental, appetite or sheer wantonness!

✦ *Food for Thought* ✦

In 2009, animal activists in Finland entered pig farms and shot videos of the horrific conditions in which pigs were being kept. The video was aired just before Christmas to create awareness among the people, as ham is the seasonal favourite in Christmas meals. A court in Salo recently acquitted Saila Kivelä and her fellow activists – who had shot the December 2009 video material – of all charges of aggravated defamation.

"The pig is an intelligent animal, which in many ways resembles the dog. In intensive piggeries the tiny shoats are lively and playful at first but soon become apathetic," said Saila Kivelä. "If dogs were being treated this way, nobody would say that they are being treated well. The well being of production animals is not the same thing as the well being of pets."

"Partly the aim is to remind people of where the ham originates. People's choices exercise an effect on animal production. Hopefully everybody will draw their own conclusions based on the videos," Kivelä observed.

– News Report from Finland

Dessert

Intellectually, human beings and animals may be different, but it's pretty obvious that animals have a rich emotional life and that they feel joy and pain. It's easy to forget the connection between a hamburger and the cow it came from. But I forced myself to acknowledge the fact that every time I ate a hamburger, a cow had ceased to breathe and moo and walk around.

– Moby, American Musician,
Song writer and DJ

CHAPTER FIVE

WHY GO VEGETARIAN?

Naivedya:

He who permits the slaughter of an animal, he who cuts it up, he who kills it, he who buys or sells meat, he who cooks it, he who serves it up, and he who eats it, must all be considered as the slayers of the animal. There is no greater sinner than that man who though not worshiping the gods or the ancestors, seeks to increase the bulk of his own flesh by the flesh of other beings.

— Manu-samhita 5.51-52

Invocation:

Think of the sufferings of animals in the name of civilisation or science!
Vivisection claims the authority of many a scientist.
Meat-diet is regarded as the diet of the refined, civilised man!
Who will save the animals?

— Sadhu Vaswani

Apertif:

Vegetarian food leaves a deep impression on our nature. If the whole world adopts vegetarianism, it can change the destiny of humankind.

— Albert Einstein

✦ Starters ✦

One of the guests invited to dinner at Leo Tolstoy's residence insisted that she should be served meat, and would not tolerate a vegetarian meal which Tolstoy recommended. When she was escorted to the dining table by Tolstoy, she found a live chicken tied to her chair. "What is the meaning of this?" she demanded sternly.

The great writer replied politely, "Dear lady, as you know, my conscience forbids me to kill any living creature. Tonight, you are the only guest at my table who is taking flesh food. I would be deeply obliged to you, if you could undertake the killing of the creature you wish to consume."

It is reported that the dinner that night was strictly vegetarian for all the guests!

✦ Main Course ✦

In earlier chapters, we spoke of the noble ideal of *ahimsa* and the concept of the inviolable sanctity of all life – the basic principles on which vegetarianism is founded. We also saw that inflicting pain on any creature was against the spirit of *ahimsa*. How is it possible that I avoid food of violence in my diet, but condone the cruelty meted out to animals in processes like vivisection, experimentation, drug testing, etc? How can I spray myself with expensive perfume which I know contains extracts from the innards of endangered species like sperm whales? How can I ingest so-called life-saving drugs which actually contain substances of animal origin? How can I support the policies and practices of companies which thrive on animal experimentation? How can I enjoy entertainments like the circus where caged animals are subjected to cruel confinement and treatment?

These are questions which every vegetarian, every believer in the principle of *ahimsa* must ask – and attempt to answer for himself or herself. You might remember too, I spoke of what is called a true vegetarian lifestyle: as I said, a true vegetarian causes no harm, pain or injury to any living creature. In the Hindu way of life, we believe that all creation is a manifestation of the Divine; each creature is a spark of the Divine Flame; even as we revere the Divine, it is incumbent upon us to show reverence to all forms of life. In the One Family of creation, animals and birds are man's younger brothers and sisters. How then can we exploit them and cause them harm and injury? Therefore, the true vegetarian carefully refrains from causing injury and pain to any living creature in any manner, direct or indirect.

When we talk about a vegetarian lifestyle, we invariably tend to think of our diet: true, vegetarian food is perhaps the toughest choice that 'converts' must make. Indeed, much of this book is also concerned with the benefits of a vegetarian diet. But in an era when awareness and sensitivity are growing, we need to realise that a vegetarian lifestyle, a way of life that is based on *ahimsa*, now embraces several aspects and issues in which we have to choose right; these include the following:

1. Cosmetics, creams, personal hygiene products, perfumes and deodorants
2. Accessories, handbags, wallets, attire
3. Footwear
4. Luggage
5. Household cleaners, disinfectants, sprays, etc.
6. Pesticides and mosquito/fly repellents
7. Medicines and health care products
8. Processed and manufactured food products like

biscuits, cakes, baked goods, chocolates and ice cream, and *mithai* bought from shops.

9. Reading labels, understanding sources and origins of products

10. Livelihood and investment options

Perhaps some of you are beginning to wonder, "What have all these things got to do with vegetarianism?" The answer is that the true vegetarian needs to be aware, sensitive and proactive in avoiding, preventing cruelty to animals in any manner, by becoming well-informed on all the above issues.

Devil's advocates (who are a plenty in every intellectual endeavour) argue that this kind of non-injury or non-violence is simply not practical in daily life. Some years ago, I met a few of the representatives of the admirable Beauty Without Cruelty association, who are carrying on a valiant struggle against such cruelty to animals. They told me how it was becoming increasingly difficult to avoid animal-origin ingredients and cruelty-free processes even in products which we assumed to be totally vegetarian. But the voices of protest have not been in vain! In the last decade alone, several world-renowned cosmetic companies have stopped testing their products on animals, and proclaim this fact on their labels. Similarly, others carry the affirmation that their products are free from any ingredient of animal origin. Above all, countless activists and movements throughout the world are keeping an ever-vigilant eye on products and processes to ensure that no harm is caused to living creatures in their manufacture, as also to warn the general public against the use of such products.

As for the practicality or impracticality of the choice of non-violence as a way of life, I believe with Mahatma Gandhi, that human nature is intrinsically good; and good, right-thinking people will always be there, who prefer the way of non-injury to violence and harm. If such a choice is difficult to make and to sustain, well, as Gandhiji points out, all things that are worthwhile and valuable are difficult to achieve and sustain! As idealists and seekers of transformation, we must continue to uphold the belief that non-violence is conceivable, practical, and desirable; we only have to find the best way to propagate it and ensure its awareness and acceptance in the world we live in.

To my mind, *ahimsa* is not a 'policy' that one can follow or drop strategically; it is a supreme virtue which is fundamental to my *dharma* – my duty and morality. I would not agonise over its practicality or impracticality any more than I would question the possibility of self-realisation. And ultimately, I believe in the justice of the principle of *ahimsa*: it is morally and ethically wrong to inflict cruelty and pain on any living creature, directly or indirectly: it is this rightness, this sense of innate justice that will eventually make the cause of vegetarianism successful.

In the sections that follow, we shall examine why Vegetarianism is the right choice for us – on grounds of religion, philosophy, tradition and culture, as well as on grounds of good health, disease prevention, and in the interests of environmental protection, economics and aesthetics.

✦ *Food for Thought* ✦

In the name of scientific enlightenment, biology students have been dissecting animals for generations. For some, the procedure has solved some of the mysteries of life. For others, it was simply disgusting. Either way, it was mandatory. But, a rebellion has been growing in the science laboratories of the nation's schools as a growing number of students refuse to dissect animals, usually on the grounds that it is inhumane.

"Animals are just as alive as we are," said Jasmine Dixon, an Indianapolis 11th-grader who refused to dissect any animal in biology. "They have feelings. They have families."

Many states have been pondering bills that would allow students to complete alternative work in science if they oppose dissection. Such laws have been enacted in California, Florida, Maryland, New York and Pennsylvania. The Illinois House of Representatives recently passed a similar bill, which is being debated in the state Senate. Without such a law, students who refuse to dissect animals routinely face sanctions, or lowered grades, from science teachers.

Indeed, the Anti-Vivisection Society sponsors a toll-free number for students facing academic troubles for their opposition to dissection (1-800-922-3764).

Humane groups say lessons can be taught just as effectively with plastic models or computer simulations, usually at a saving of costs. But some scientists see it differently. "Sometimes there just isn't any substitute for looking at the real thing," said Jose Bonner, an associate professor of biology at Indiana University in Bloomington.

The issue has become more heated in recent years as more and more young people refuse to eat meat or use animal products. The debate over dissection flared in 1987 when a 15-year-old California girl, Jennifer Graham, refused to dissect an animal and sued her school district for not allowing her to complete some alternative project. She complained that animals were being needlessly killed simply to be used for such projects. Miss Graham became something of a celebrity, often called "the frog girl", who had the courage to stand up to the schools in her defense of defenseless animals. The public backed her, and lawmakers in California ultimately passed legislation protecting students who held such views, the first law of its kind in the United States.

– New York Times News Service

P.S. I feel it must be recorded here with pride that in the year 2002, the Sadhu Vaswani Mission's St. Mira's College opened its Science Section over forty years after the inception of the college. The reason for this delay was that until then, dissection was compulsory in the biology laboratory. Once the government and the educational authorities reverted this policy and permitted teaching of biology through models, the College Management went ahead with the Science Division, which had been a long standing demand of many parents and students.

This has only proved my belief that it is possible to live and learn – without cruelty!

Dessert

The Brown Dog affair was a political controversy about vivisection that raged in Edwardian England from 1903 until 1910. It involved the infiltration of University of London medical lectures by Swedish women activists, pitched battles between medical students and the police, police protection for the statue of a dog, a libel trial at the Royal Courts of Justice, and the establishment of a Royal Commission to investigate the use of animals in experiments. The affair became a cause célèbre that reportedly divided the country.

The controversy was triggered by allegations that, in February 1903, William Bayliss of the Department of Physiology at University College London had performed illegal dissection before an audience of 60 medical students on a brown terrier dog—adequately anaesthetised, according to Bayliss and his team; conscious and struggling, according to the Swedish activists. The procedure was condemned as cruel and unlawful by the National Anti-Vivisection Society. Bayliss, whose research on dogs led to the discovery of hormones, was outraged by the assault on his reputation. He sued for libel and won.

Anti-vivisectionists commissioned a bronze statue of the dog as a memorial, unveiled in Battersea in 1906, but medical students were angered by its provocative plaque — "Men and women of England, how long shall these things be?" — leading to frequent vandalism of the memorial and the need for a 24-hour police guard against the so-called "anti-doggers". On December 10, 1907, 1,000 anti-doggers marched through central London, clashing with suffragettes, trade unionists, and 400 police officers in Trafalgar Square, one of a series of battles known as the Brown Dog riots.

In March 1910, tired of the constant controversy, Battersea Council sent four workers accompanied by 120 police officers to remove the statue under cover of darkness, after which it was allegedly melted down by the council's blacksmith, despite a 20,000-strong petition in its favour. A new statue of the brown dog was commissioned by anti-vivisection groups over 70 years later, and was erected in Battersea Park in 1985.

– The Independent , London

CHAPTER SIX

BENEFITS OF VEGETARIANISM

Naivedya:

Those high-souled persons who desire beauty, faultlessness of limbs, long life, under-standing, mental and physical strength and memory should abstain from acts of injury.

– Mahabharata 18.115.8

Invocation:

Fresh, natural fruits and vegetables add joy and zest to life. 'Dead' foods only make your stomach a graveyard for diseased carcasses.

– J.P. Vaswani

Apertif:

I have no doubt that it is a part of the destiny of the human race, in its gradual improvement, to leave off eating animals, as surely as the savage tribes have left off eating each other when they came in contact with the more civilised.

– Henry David Thoreau, Walden

✦ Starters ✦

Bernard Shaw, Nobel Laureate and an outstanding playwright of the early Twentieth Century, became a vegetarian when he was twenty-five years old, after hearing a lecture by H.F. Lester. He remained a staunch practitioner of vegetarianism till the very end of his life and attributed his good health to his vegetarianism. He found it not only economical but also aesthetically more satisfying.

He firmly believed that vegetarianism would elevate the quality of human beings. "I do not want to make my stomach a graveyard of dead animals." he stated categorically, adding for good measure, "If life is offered to me on condition of eating beefsteaks I would say death is better than cannibalism." In 1901, recalling his conversion to vegetarianism, he said, "I was a cannibal for twenty-five years. For the rest I have been a vegetarian." As a staunch vegetarian, he was a firm anti-vivisectionist and antagonistic to cruel sports for the remainder of his life. The belief in the immorality of eating animals was one of the Fabian causes close to his heart and is frequently a theme in his plays and prefaces. His position, succinctly stated, was, "A man of my spiritual intensity does not eat corpses."

✦ Main Course ✦

Good Health and Vegetarianism

When members of our Sadhu Vaswani Centre in Singapore approached a few of their Chinese friends to observe November 25 as a "Meatless day", they met with the shocked response: "But how will we be able to live without taking meat for a whole day?"

They got the shock of their lives when they learnt that though I have lived for over ninety years, I had not tasted meat even once. And when they met me and spoke to me they were amazed.

Things have changed today. An ever increasing number of people all over the world are turning to vegetarianism as a "way of life" which leads to health and strength of the body, mind and soul. Scientific research has shown that a flesh-diet has adverse effects on health.

Heart disease continues to be the number one killer of humanity. It is strongly linked with high blood levels of cholesterol. Cholesterol is found largely in animal products. And the people are beginning to realise, more and more, the health benefits of a low-fat vegetarian diet.

Heart disease is also linked with high blood pressure. Research studies have shown that people who eat a vegetarian diet, tend to have not only lower levels of blood cholesterol but also lower blood pressure than those consuming food of violence (flesh, fish, fowl, etc.) Animal products, it has been proved, contain high saturated fat, which the body converts into cholesterol.

Recent researches have also indicated that a low-fat vegetarian diet helps cure as well as prevent heart and other diseases, including cancers of breasts, colon and prostrate. This is because, as nutritionists tell us, the high amount of animal fat present in meat, dairy and other animal products may be probable factors leading to increase of diabetes mellitus, obesity, colorectal cancer, high blood pressure and coronary artery disease, which are all linked directly or indirectly to heart diseases.

What many people do not realise is that besides these diseases, the following are also either prevented, or even cured by low-fat vegetarian diet:

1. Strokes and heart disease
2. Stomach and colon cancer
3. Gallstones
4. Hypertension
5. Endometrial cancer
6. Kidney disease & stones

7. Breast cancer, prostrate cancer, pancreatic cancer, cervical cancer and ovarian cancer

8. Hypoglycaemia

9. Peptic ulcers

10. Constipation

11. Hiatal hernias

12. Diverticulosis

13. Salmonellosis

14. Trichinosis

15. Osteoporosis

16. Hemorrhoids

17. Asthma

18. Irritable colon syndrome

(Sources: The Shocking Truth And Statistics About Your Food! - A report published widely on the internet by Janice Hoo)

A number of people are under the impression that they and their children cannot be strong unless they eat food of violence. Meat gives strength to the body, they say. Without meat, the body becomes weak and a prey to many diseases.

As an answer to this query, the example is given of the elephant which is one of the biggest and strongest animals in the world: and the elephant is a pure vegetarian. What of the lion? Someone will ask. The elephant cannot match his strength against that of the lion. True, but the lion has destructive strength; while the strength of an elephant can be used in the service of humanity. The elephant carries huge logs of wood from one place to another. Can you make a lion do likewise? Perhaps yes, but at the risk of your own life! It was Shakespeare who said, "O, it is excellent to have a giant's strength, but it is tyrannous to use it like a giant."

What is it about flesh food that is disease-causing? Every medical research report on a healthy diet will make it plain to you:

1. Meat is high in unsaturated fats that lead to an increase in cholesterol levels in the blood. Dr. Christian Barnard, a cardiac expert, tells us: "People who become fat by overeating animal fats are more likely to develop coronary heart disease than people whose obesity is caused by an over indulgence in foods that do not elevate the blood cholesterol level."

2. Studies have shown a strong correlation between the incidence of colon cancer and meat consumption. Livestock with cancerous diseases are often used for meat production, perhaps because the disease has not been detected. In some cases, tumours are simply cut out for the carcass to pass inspection as 'wholesome' meat. Such diseases are

simply 'passed over' to the consumer.

3. Meat, which is after all flesh from the dead body of an animal, is often full of bacteria that are not found in vegetables. Dr. Walden M.D. an expert meat inspector says, "According to the Bureau of Labour, the poultry processing industry is the third most hazardous, even ahead of steelworkers and bulldozer operators, due to the occupational hazard of disease from bacterially infected flesh." He adds that many vets in the U.S. simply advise their clients in cattle farms to "ship off" to the slaughterhouse, an animal that is found to be infected with disease. Salmonella and E-Coliare two of the bacterial contaminants in swine and cattle.

4. Nitrogenous wastes in flesh food put tremendous strain on the kidneys of people who eat a carnivorous diet.

5. Recent research has also indicated that for many of the same reasons, vegetarians are at a lower risk for osteoporosis. It is thought that animal products force calcium out of the body, thereby promoting bone loss.

Quite apart from the above, it has been found that the anatomical structure and general body functions of homo sapiens is totally different from our carnivorous animal brethren, proving that man was designed and created to be a vegetarian in diet:

1. We have an extremely long intestinal canal which is actually ten to twelve times the length of the body, forming a winding, intricate route, which is poorly adapted for the digestion and elimination of flesh food. On the other hand, natural carnivores (i.e. meat-eating animals as the wolf, lion, hyena, and cat) all possess a digestive tract only three times the length of the animal's body, which are meant to eliminate rapidly, decaying substances such as meat in a very short time.

2. All carnivores have powerful jaws and long fangs — the sharp, elongated canine teeth which are meant for spearing and tearing flesh. We may study the fangs and jaws of the modern tiger, to realise the dental equipment necessary for a true carnivore. Dr. A. S. Romer, Professor Emeritus of Zoology at Harvard, has written that "the canines are long and pointed stabbing weapons in all flesh eaters."

   We humans have no such dental provisions. What we do have are sharp incisor teeth and very well developed molar teeth for the biting, grinding and chewing of vegetables, fruits, and nuts.

3. The great Swedish naturalist, Karl von Linne' (Linnaeus) tells us: "Man's structure, external and internal, compared with that of other animals,

shows that fruit and succulent vegetables constitute his natural food."

4. Most carnivores perspire through their tongues, as their skin lacks pores. We can easily see this happening with dogs, who pant with their tongues hanging out, to reduce their body heat and keep cool. Being nocturnal hunters, they sleep in the heat of the day. On the other hand, herbivores or vegetarian animals normally function during the day, and their skin has millions of pores, through which they freely perspire to regulate their body temperature.

5. Our stomach does not have the ruminant's many chambers for digesting grass, nor the extremely high hydrochloric acid content of a carnivore's (very useful in a cat, for example, to digest fur and bones from a mouse).

We may conclude therefore, that humans were not meant to eat flesh food. We must remember too, that all other carnivores kill their own prey and consume the flesh thereof; our non-vegetarian brothers and sisters prefer to do their killing by proxy. Their meat is slaughtered elsewhere, and cleaned, dressed, baked, boiled or fried before it is 'presented' at the table. It is also suitably 'tenderised' and dressed with sauces, gravies, herbs and spices.

Finally, the question of longevity: although I am

qualified by virtue of my own age to stand testimony to the connection between a vegetarian diet and longevity, I refrain from doing so out of modesty. Instead, I end with the words of Bernard Shaw, who called himself a second 'Mahatma':

The average age of a meat-eater is 63. I am on the verge of 85 and still work as hard as ever. I have lived quite long enough and I am trying to die; but I simply cannot do it. A single beefsteak would finish me; but I cannot bring myself to swallow it. I am oppressed with a dread of living forever. That is the only disadvantage of vegetarianism.

Environmental Concerns and the Economics of Vegetarianism

As we have seen in earlier sections, people have chosen vegetarianism as the right option for different reasons and different concerns, over the centuries. While scriptural principles/religious teachings, faith, tradition and culture have kept the flame of *ahimsa* alive for most Indian vegetarians, westerners have been increasingly turning towards a vegetarian or vegan lifestyle based on their growing concern for sustainable development in what seems to bean unjust world order. In a sense, this involves awareness of politics, economics, market realities of meat production and third world development issues. However, all these issues do not dilute people's passionate commitment to the cause of vegetarianism. Thus, we now have two distinct groups of people practising a vegetarian lifestyle: those who are born and brought up as vegetarians and are deeply committed to the cause on grounds of faith and innate belief; and those who have been born and brought up in a flesh food eating home environment and have deliberately and consciously converted to vegetarianism on grounds of justice, ethics, morality and conviction of right and wrong.

If any of you are wondering how economics,

ecology, third world development and vegetarianism are related, let me demystify the issue. As I said earlier, interconnectedness is a theme that constantly underlines the growing concern for the environment and the future of our planet. We know that building a dam across a river somewhere upstream is going to displace, disrupt and affect the lives of people living hundreds of miles away. We know too, that we cannot shrug our shoulders and feign indifference when Amazon forests are being felled or when growing industrialisation begins to melt the snow cap in the South or North Poles. Sooner or later, it will become an issue of global warming which affects us all.

A *New York Times* feature article, "The Meat Guzzler" points out that factory farming or intensive animal production is environmentally unsustainable on three counts: 1. Pollution of water resources 2. Degradation and desertification of vast tracts of land that are continually used for grazing and 3. Wasteful and extra vagantuse of fuels and water. According to *Livestock's Long Shadow*, an FAO report, the meat industry contributes about 18 percent of global greenhouse-gas emissions, including carbon dioxide, methane and nitrous oxide. In America alone, more than one-third of the fossil fuels produced are used to raise animals for food.

If my readers are wondering why we have suddenly got into the realm of production figures, let me inform you: meat production and meat consumption are no longer market issues related to individual choice or particular nations. They have become crucial issues that affect global concerns like the problems of hunger, malnutrition, famine and infant mortality involving vast populations across the world. Let me quote a few experts who have written extensively on the subject: Environmental vegetarianism is based on the belief that the production of meat and animal products for mass consumption, especially through factory farming, is environmentally unsustainable or otherwise harmful. Recent research strongly supports these concerns. According to a 2006 United Nations initiative, the livestock industry is one of the largest contributors to environmental degradation worldwide, and modern practices of raising animals for food contributes on a "massive scale" to air and water pollution, land degradation, climate change, and loss of biodiversity. The initiative concluded that "the livestock sector emerges as one of the top two or three most significant contributors to the most serious environmental problems, at every scale from local to global."

In addition, animal agriculture has been pointed out as one of the largest sources of greenhouse gases-responsible for 18 percent of the world's greenhouse gas emissions as measured in CO_2 equivalents. By comparison, all of the world's transportation (including all cars, trucks, buses, trains, ships, and planes) emits 13.5 percent of the CO_2. Animal farming produces 65 percent of human-related nitrous oxide and 37 percent of all human-induced methane. The habitat for wildlife provided by large industrial monoculture farms is very poor, and modern industrial agriculture has been considered a threat to biodiversity compared with farming practices such as organic farming, permaculture, arable, pastoral, and rainfed agriculture. Animals fed on grain, and those that rely on grazing need farmore water than grain crops. According to the USDA, growing the crops necessary to feed farmed animals requires nearly half of the United States' water supply and 80 percent of its agricultural land. Additionally, animals raised for food in the U.S. consume 90 percent of the soy crop, 80 percent of the corn crop, and a total of 70 percent of its grain.

Just imagine! Good food grains grown by subsidised farmers in the US are sold at inflated prices to cattle farmers who feed them to livestock, while millions of people go to bed hungry everyday! Pigs, cows, chickens, sheep and hapless humans are all competing for the same grains!

Here is what we are told about the World Food Crisis: According to UN sources, over 50% of the world's population is hungry or malnourished; among these, nearly half have less than barely enough food on which to survive. Hunger, we are told, kills more people than AIDS, malaria and tuberculosis combined. World population growth is outpacing food production, particularly with the four crops that provide the bulk of the world's nutrition: wheat, rice, corn and soyabeans. In 2008, the World Food Program called the situation a "silent tsunami" of world hunger. Are we using the land in the most practical and productive manner to solve the world food crisis? Most experts agree that meat production is a wasteful use of our precious land and water resources. When we feed grains to animals, food is being wasted! As Erik Marcus observes, "It is anotoriously inefficient and wasteful process by which grain is converted to flesh". It takes about thirteen pounds of grain to produce a pound of flesh! But this is not all. Intensive animal farming, cattle ranching etc. have ravaged several acres of prime agricultural land. And the seafood lovers' craze for fish have ruined the world's oceans.

Such is the skewed economics of food trade that a well-researched article tells us:

> It is a great modern tragedy that today the have-nations are even importing tremendous quantities of foodstuffs from have not nations; England, for example, imports every year from India, some 100,000 tons of oil-seed cake material which is very high in protein. Methods have been developed already, to extract this high quality protein from the oil-seed cake material, for human

consumption. But the 100,000 tons per year of oil-seed cake material are used to help feed the vast quantities of factory- farmed food animals of Britain, so that the British people may continue to enjoy their high standard of dietary cholesterol! Similarly, Europe takes in from Africa comparable amounts of such materials, for use as food for animals that are destined for ultimate slaughter. The amounts involved would apparently at least make up the protein deficiencies in these poorer areas of the world.

— Facts of Vegetarianism,
American Vegetarian Society

There are several reasons for this food crisis; and as individuals, there is not a lot we can do about factors like misplaced global trade policies and national mismanagement, the diversion of crops to fuel, black marketeering etc. But there is one thing we can all do: it is in our power to change our own diet.

In terms of food economics, the production of plant foods per unit of land is usually more than ten times that achieved when we cycle this precious nutritious source through animals before we ourselves consume the same! In simple terms, producing animal based food is typically much less efficient than the direct harvesting of grains, vegetables, legumes, seeds and fruits for direct human consumption. Dennis Avery, Director of the Centre for Global Food Issues, puts it simply, when he tells us, "The world must create five billion vegans in the next several decades, or triple its total farm output without using more land."

Economic Vegetarians believe in simple living. According to the World watch Institute, "Massive reductions in meat consumption in industrial nations will ease the health care burden while improving public health; declining livestock herds will take pressure off rangelands and grainlands, allowing the agricultural resource base to rejuvenate. As populations grow, lowering meat consumption worldwide will allow more efficient use of declining per capital and water resources, while at the same time making grain more affordable to the world's chronically hungry."

I end with the words of Albert Einstein: "Nothing will benefit human health and increase the chances of survival of life on earth as much as the evolution to a vegetarian diet."

✦ *Food for Thought* ✦

The wrong food choices put a strain on our environment.

It is leading to our own endangerment.

Are we all crazy? Are we insane?

When we destroy the earth, then who will we blame?

Are we in time? Is it too late?

Have we committed ourselves? Is the damage too great?

Mother Earth is dying. It's just not right!

She needs our help. We have to fight!

Some people wonder: "what's all the fuss?"

Well, we are killing the very planet that sustains us!

"Ignorance is bliss" is what some people choose to believe.

Destruction of mother earth is what ignorance will achieve.

This is really quite serious.

Our ignorance is actually killing us.

– Jeff Rogers

Ethics, Morality and Vegetarianism

It is said that the Universal Law common to all religions is the golden rule: Do as you would be done by. I feel there is one other golden rule which is even more basic than this: it is the fundamental law of humanity: Live and let live.

Gurudev Sadhu Vaswani expressed this idea in the mystic, poetic way that was so characteristic of him: "For me, not to love bird and beast would be not to love the Lord!" An angel of compassion and sensitivity, he was nevertheless forthright in condemning animal slaughter. "O, the sin of daily slaughter in our heartless cities!" he exclaimed, more in sorrow than in anger, adding words that will continue to touch the conscience of humanity for generations to come: "Believe me, meat-eating will one day be condemned as murder!"

Once, a group of educated Indians tried to tell Gurudev Sadhu Vaswani that the methods of the modern slaughterhouse were 'humane' and 'painless'. "As well might we speak of humane murder!" was his reply to them. His uncompromising, unceasing, persistent call to the world was, "Stop all slaughter!"

Prof. Howard Moore, an American zoologist, a writer of several books and advocate of vegetarianism and the humane treatment of animals, tells us:

A universe is, indeed, to be pitied whose dominating inhabitants are so unconscious and so ethically embryonic that they make life a commodity, mercy a disease, and systematic massacre a pastime and a profession... Yes, do as you would be done by– and not to the dark man and the white woman alone, but to the sorrelhorse and the grey squirrel as well; not to creatures of your own anatomy alone, but to all creatures... Do to beings below as you would be done by beings above you.

They are our fellow mortals. They came out of the same mysterious womb of the past, are passing through the same dream, and are destined to the same melancholy end as we ourselves. Let us be kind and merciful to them...

Live and let live. Do more. Live and help live. Do to beings below you as you would be done by beings above you.

When we read Prof. Moore's writings now, it is obvious that his thinking was well ahead of his time. His attitude and approach to animal rights fore shadows the work of later and more well known activists like Peter Singer, of whom we spoke earlier. Because animals are sentient Moore argues that they too should have the same rights as human beings to be treated in ways that limit their suffering and maximises their well-being.

In this context, any talk of 'lower' animals or

creatures made to be food to man, sounds hollow, does it not?

It was Mahatma Gandhi who stated this in clear-cut terms:

> To my mind, the life of a lamb is no less precious than that of a human being. I should be unwilling to take the life of a lamb for the sake of the human body.
>
> I want to realise brotherhood or identity not merely with the beings called human, but I want to realise identity with all life, even with such things as crawl upon earth.

The *jiva,* or the life-principle, Gurudev Sadhu Vaswani saw as the will to-live, which is manifested in all creation. Thus *himsa* to him was nothing but "the harmony of my will-to-live with the will-to-live of other creatures". It was in this belief that he asserted, *"Ahimsa* is profound surrender of myself for the sake of Life in others...I must do nothing to wound the *jiva in* other creatures. I must be true to the principle of the will-to-live."

It is not only ancient Indian wisdom which urges the ethical principle of live-and let-live. The Cherokee Indians have their myth of a golden age of harmony when man lived in perfect peace with his fellow creatures and all of nature, and men, animals and plants could actually speak to each other. A Chieftain of this tribe said to the new white settlers on his soil,

"...the deer, the horse, the great eagle, these are our brothers. The rocky crests, the juices in the meadows, the body heat of the pony and man–all belong to the same family... The White Man must treat the beasts of this land as his brothers."

In Greece too, the philosopher Empedocles wrote of a "golden age of love...when no altar was wet with shameful slaughter". To Empedocles, man's primal and original sin was the slaughter of animals. In fact, most ancient cultures say that man fell from his state of grace, harmony and innocence when he started to kill for food.

Taoism holds all Nature as sacred, and this view favours vegetarianism. According to the Tao, the process of meat production tends to be too aggressive, involving extreme and unnecessary violence and having a negative and destructive impact on the environment.

Here are some of the rules put into practice by Taoist monks of yore:

1. Thou shalt not whip or beat domestic animals.
2. Thou shalt not intentionally or carelessly crush beneath thy feet insects and animals.
3. Thou shalt not take delight in fishhooks or arrows in order to get amusement.
4. Thou shalt not catch birds and animals in

nets or snares.

5. Thou shalt not alarm or scare away birds sitting in their nests.

6. Thou shalt not pluck flowers or pull up grass without reason.

7. Thou shalt not cut down trees or burn hillside woods.

Supreme Master Suma Ching Hai has also given her opinion on the relationship of vegetarianism and enlightenment by saying, "To be completely enlightened and to keep the state of happiness at all times, we should grant happiness to all beings well in a complete way. Give them no fear, give them no threatening atmosphere wherever you walk, and then you'll experience free feelings and a very, very loving atmosphere always around you. That is the more complete enlightenment."

Most vegetarians in western countries have avoided flesh food for ethical reasons: the first of these is the opposition to all killing in general; the second is the unspeakable cruelty and pain inflicted on animals in factory farming and modern abattoirs. If it is wrong to kill human beings, they argue, it must be equally wrong to kill sentient beings like animals.

Flesh food eaters counter this belief by stating that on moral, intellectual and cultural grounds, animals can never be equated with human beings. They add, for good measure, that what applies to animals must also apply to plants, and that vegetarians 'kill' plants to satisfy their cravings. "Vegetarians say they don't eat meat because they don't want to kill," they point out, "but eating plants is taking life too." But here too, they operate by double standards that borders on moral hypocrisy. While they insist that eating animals is not morally different from eating plants, they nevertheless draw a distinction between animals consumed for meat and pet animals like cats, dogs and horses. Thus while they find it healthy, ethical and civilised to consume sheep, lambs, pigs and chickens, they are horrified by the moral repugnancy of eating dogs or cats! To put it simply, "Some animals are more equal than others"!

Abolitionists go well beyond the claims of animal welfare activists: they feel that reforms in animal welfare are not enough to protect animals. To them any form of proprietary rights over animals is not acceptable, for it makes people comfortable about their 'rights' to use animals. "We don't want bigger cages: we want empty cages," is their cry. Their aim is to bring about a moral and ethical paradigm shift whereby animals cannot be regarded as things to be owned and used. For them, veganism is a matter of fundamental moral justice.

Prof. Tom Regan, an ardent abolitionist, tells us in his essay, "*Animal Rights and the Myth of 'Humane' Treatment*":

The other animals humans eat, use in science, hunt, trap, and exploit in a variety of ways, have a life of their own that is of importance to them apart from their utility to us. They are not only in the world, they are aware of it. What happens to them matters to them. Each has a life that fares better or worse for the one whose life it is.

That life includes a variety of biological, individual, and social needs. The satisfaction of these needs is a source of pleasure, their frustration or abuse, a source of pain. In these fundamental ways the non human animals in labs and on farms, for example, are the same as human beings. And so it is that the ethics of our dealings with them, and with one another, must acknowledge the same fundamental moral principles.

At its deepest level, human ethics is based on the independent value of the individual. The moral worth of any human being is not to be measured by how useful that person is in advancing the interests of other human beings. To treat human beings in ways that do not honour their independent value is to violate that most basic of human rights: the right of each person to be treated with respect.

The philosophy of animal rights demands only that logic be respected. For any argument that plausibly explains the independent value of human beings implies that other animals have this same value, and have it equally. And any argument that plausibly explains the right of humans to be treated with respect also implies that these other animals have this same right, and have it equally, too.

In ancient India, people were enjoined to offer prayers not only for creatures on this earth, but for all living things in all the worlds. Here is one such prayer that Gurudev Sadhu Vaswani loved:

In all lands may all the sufferings of living beings come to an end!

May the beaten be freed from blows!

May those who are threatened with death be restored to life!

May those who are in tribulation become free from all pain!

May those who suffer from hunger and thirst receive food and drink in abundance!

May the blind see and the deaf hear and women bearing children give birth painlessly!

May sounds of pain be heard nowhere in this world!

May living creatures avoid the low way!

May the torment and anguish of those who dwell in the narkalok come to an end!

May the ghosts be happy!

May all living beings be liberated from the cycle of reincarnation!

Killing animals for food, experimenting on animals, hunting for entertainment or commerce, capturing young animals for fur, imprisoning them in cages, tormenting them to learn tricks for our entertainment, and ignoring the rights of animals to life are all cruel, inhuman practices and must be condemned by all people who respect ethics and morality. We all know that we can be the change we want, if only we decide to start with a change in our own food habits!

"In a universe which embraces all types of life and consciousness and all material forms through which these manifest, nothing which is ethically wrong can ever be scientifically right; that in an integrated cosmos of spirit and matter one law must pervade all levels and all planes. This is the basic principle upon which the whole case against vivesection rests. Cicero summed it up in the four words: 'No cruelty is useful'." —

M. Beddow Bayly (MRCS, LRCP England, member of the National Anti-Vaccination League and the Animal Defence and Anti-Vivisection Society)

Philosophy and Vegetarianism

I would not go so far as to argue that a vegetarian is more philosophically inclined than a flesh food eater. But those who advocate a universal policy of non-violence and urge people to stop all killing definitely adopt a more morally and ethically positive position than those who justify animal slaughter. Philosophy, in this sense, may be defined as the system of values by which one lives. It is also a critical analysis of the beliefs and assumptions of a particular system. Thus vegetarianism is a philosophy of life with the following assumptions:

1. All forms of life are equal and must be revered. (The principle of reverence for all life)

2. Animals are not resources to be exploited at man's will– for food, attire, entertainment or sport.

3. As human beings, we are a part of the world of nature, not its owners or masters.

4. No life is superfluous, and we have no right to take a life away, since we can never give it back.

5. There is no 'hierarchy' in living beings that justifies the killing of certain creatures.

6. Cruelty, violence and infliction of pain and suffering on another being is abominable and morally repugnant.

7. Peace, harmony and progress cannot be achieved at the expense of violence, cruelty and killing.

8. Compassion and benevolence are high humane values to be extended to all living beings.

9. The Universe is inter-connected. Everything that we do touches the world around us in one way or another.

   Each one of us is responsible for the protection and well being of the environment in which we live.

10. The prime value of mindfulness, compassion and reverence for all life should override all other aspects of custom, culture, tradition, taste and convenience. Daniel Dombrowski tells us in his book, *The Philosophy of Vegetarianism,* that it is wrong for modern vegetarians to appropriate the idea of vegetarianism to themselves. According to him, philosophical vegetarianism was already an idea with a thousand year old history in ancient Greece, advocated by great minds like Pythagoras, Empedocles, Theophrastus, Plutarch and perhaps Socrates and Plato as well. For some reason, the idea died out and was revived several centuries later, as modern vegetarian philosophy.

Since the 1970s a great deal of literature and research has been published on the subject, not to mention the fact that millions of people worldwide have taken to vegetarianism for ethical, moral and medical reasons.

Ancient philosophers saw the vegetarian way of life as arête – virtuous and of excellence. As Dombrowski tells us:

> Ancient vegetarians had several bases for their stance: (1) a mythological belief in a past vegetarian golden age; (2) a faith in transmigration, which led them to spare animals in the belief that animals were, or would become, human beings; (3) a concern that flesh-eating was injurious to the health of either body or soul – the former being tied to ancient medical thought, and the latter concern associated with a more general commitment to moderation or asceticism. But it will also be seen that (4) there was among the ancients a concern for animals themselves – in as much as animals either suffer before they are killed or are deprived of their life even if killed painlessly, and in that we can lead healthy lives on vegetal food, eating meat is cruel and ought to be avoided.

The scholar admits however, that if modern vegetarianism was a phoenix that arose out of its own ashes in the West, the East has had a long and unbroken tradition for over 2000 years!

In the West, perhaps the Judeo-Christian tradition was responsible for justifying man's superiority and his right to 'use' animals for his benefit. It was only in the nineteenth century that the dormant philosophy was revived – on grounds of ethics, health benefits and humane treatment of animals. Notable writers and thinkers who advocated the cause of vegetarianism were the poet, Percy Bysshe Shelley, Henry Salt (whose book *Animals' Rights* was a landmark publication in vegetarian writing, a pioneering volume), and George Bernard Shaw, who admitted that he was greatly influenced by Salt.

In more recent times, vegetarianism is becoming popular on fresh grounds: concern for the environment and ecology; sustainable development; health concerns; and a reassessment of the morality of animal rights. Concerns about world poverty, hunger and malnutrition in the third world have also led to ethical preference for vegetarianism.

Activism, utilitarianism, ecology, abolitionism or animal liberation – it is futile to get too involved in philosophical differences. When it comes to vegetarianism, we should practise it whole heartedly, rather than take sides with one group or another.

Spirituality and Vegetarianism

I will be the first to agree that God is one, while the paths to reach Him are many! He is Nameless and Formless, but the devout worship Him by many names and in as many forms. I also believe firmly, that God loves each and every one of us as dearly as a Father loves his children; He does not discriminate on grounds of colour, creed or race. None of us is superior or inferior in His eyes.

But I still assert that vegetarianism, as a way of life, promotes spirituality.

I must also tell you that many of my non-vegetarian friends dismiss this as typical vegetarian propaganda!

Akemi Gaimes, a believer in real-life spirituality, once argued that vegetarians were no more spiritual than others. This, in spite of the fact that she herself was a practising vegetarian. But when she learnt more about what went into the production, processing and labelling of meat and meat products, her attitude underwent a sea-change, and she concluded: "Spirituality is about anything and everything in life. You are a spiritual being in the physical body, so you can't not be spiritual. Everything in life affects your spirituality. Your eating habit affects your spirituality, and certain choices align with spiritual evolution better than others. You can't compartmentalize spirituality and insist what you eat has nothing to do with your spirituality... So we can improve our physical health with spiritual awareness or sharpen our awareness with physical behaviour changes: physical behaviour as mundane and everyday as eating."

What do I mean by spirituality? Not an 'ideology' or a 'lifestyle' as some scholars have described it, but an effort to communicate with the Divine within us, a quest for true self-knowledge, a recognition of the living presence of the Divine all around us. It is an attempt to respond to the sacred, an attempt to seek the God within. In Hindu belief, it is an effort to perceive the vision of the One-in-all, which is the essence of *Vedanta*.

Why should a vegetarian be regarded as more spiritually inclined or spiritually evolved than a non-vegetarian? My answer to this controversial question is this: when I choose vegetarianism for economic or environmental or even charitable reasons, it becomes my ideology. But when I choose vegetarianism in the belief that all life is sacred, that my physical body is not just a mound of flesh and blood but a temple wherein dwells the immortal spirit, the *atman*, and that the same spark of Divine Life that animates the Universe and all of creation also animates me; and that the so-called lesser creatures on this planet are my younger brothers and sisters in the One Family of God's Creation – then the choice to go vegetarian becomes an affair of the spirit!

In India, there are still very many people who are born to a vegetarian lifestyle; but it must be said that if many of them continue to be vegetarian against all odds, it is in no small measure due to their innate spiritual conditioning. True, they might have been born and brought up in a strict and traditional home environment; but if they and their children have remained vegetarians as adults living on their own, their belief and adherence to their faith must be appreciated as much as we appreciate those who have tasted non-vegetarian food, but converted to a vegetarian lifestyle through personal conviction. The spiritual strength of these people needs to be acknowledged and appreciated.

I must sound a note of caution here: we tend to use the word 'spiritual' rather lightly these days. People often say for example, that they find music, dance, creative art or even gardening, deeply spiritual. I do not for a minute contest their belief; one can seek complete harmony with nature in caring for one's garden; one can identify with the Divine in music; one can forget one's physical and material sensations in finding the unity of dance or art; indeed, one can find God, even attain Liberation in the performance of one's duty, however mundane and lowly it may be. In all of these instances, the activity in question becomes a spiritual experience. In other words these activities become a perception of the sacred within us and around us. But finding relaxation or peace in an activity does not automatically make it spiritual.

Let me add, I find that the changing concepts of religion and spirituality in modern times are actually serving to broaden and deepen our understanding of the Divine. It is not going to be easy to develop a set of 'constructs' or criteria to measure spirituality! Indeed, for each one of us, spirituality will always be a deeply personal experience, an inner quest which we must take up alone, and cannot measure or define for others' benefit. Our feelings, thoughts and experiences in this regard, may be shared with others; the means and methods we adopt may also be discussed and compared. But central to the experience of spirituality is a sense of the sacred; it is this that makes vegetarianism or any other choice spiritual.

Let me give you another example: many people take to yoga and meditation these days purely for therapeutic reasons such as de-stressing, relaxation and reversing damage to the heart. I am told that yoga is also being built into exercise and gym routines nowadays. Undoubtedly yoga can help all these people very effectively: but their experience of yoga and meditation will be quite different from those who take to these as a form of *sadhana* or *abhyasa* as seekers on the path! So it is with vegetarianism.

Even those who take to vegetarian diet for medical or ideological reasons find that the food of non-violence has a cleansing and purifying effect on their system and attitude! Many of them assert that they are calmer, more relaxed, lighter and at peace with themselves. This is because vegetarian food is *saatvic* in quality – and the quality of *sattva,* enunciated by Sri Krishna Himself in the Bhagavad Gita is something special and intimately connected with the life of the spirit. When you understand the quality of *sattva* and why it needs to be cultivated, you will know why I refer to *saatvic* diet as conducive to spirituality!

The Gita tells us about the three *gunas* or qualities of Nature – what they are, how they bind man, how they operate and how we may rise above them. The three *gunas* are *sattva, rajas,* and *tamas* – in simple terms, we may translate them as purity, passion and inertia.

Sattva is the principle of truth, beauty and harmony. The *Srimad Bhagavata* tells us that *sattva* manifests itself in the quality of serenity, self-control, austerity, truthfulness, compassion, endurance, pure memory, contentment, renunciation, non-covetousness, faith, repugnance for sin etc.

In the *Gita*, Sri Krishna tells us:

When the light of wisdom streameth forth from all the gates of the body, then it may be known that *sattva* predominates.

XIV:11

Sri Krishna also mentions those qualities associated with *sattva*: fearlessness, purity of mind, steadfastness, control of the senses, sacrifice, study of the scriptures, non-violence, truthfulness, freedom from anger and freedom from envy, malice and pride.

Sattva elevates the mind, expanding our consciousness. The *buddhi* becomes radiant, and the whole personality becomes vital and joyous. One is able to rise above the narrow, restricting circumstances of the material world, and adopt a tranquil, serene, balanced attitude to life.

Whenever we experience true happiness, it is because *sattva* predominates in our life and character. Unable to realize this truth, we attribute happiness to external objects and circumstances. When we lose our sense of joy, we attribute it to the loss of these objects and circumstances. Whereas, if we knew the truth, we would work constantly to cultivate *sattva*, so that we may always feel true joy, the peace and bliss that surpasses understanding, and move forward on the path of liberation.

The Gita tells us that *sattvic* food is preferred by men of purity. It promotes integrity, intelligence, intellectual brilliance, strength, vigour, health, pleasure of physical and mental life, cheerfulness, delight and the true joy of living.

The foods which prolong life and promote purity, strength, health, joy and cheerfulness, which are sweet, soft, nourishing and agreeable, are liked by *sattvic* men.

XVII:8

The ideal diet is one that avoids *rajasic* and *tamasic* foods. You will not be surprised to know that what the ancient Hindu scriptures regarded as *sattvic* food is now held up to be the ideal food – although by other names! Experts call it high-fibre, natural, anti-oxidant etc. and we are encouraged to eat more of such foods. Basically, a vegetarian diet is the closest we can get to *sattvic* food. As for what the sages called *rajasic*, *tamasic* food – the very same foods are now labelled high-fat, high-cholesterol, carcinogenic etc. and we are warned to keep them out of our diets to the greatest extent possible!

Are all vegetarians sattvic by nature? Alas, no! But a vegetarian diet promotes *sattvic* nature. Such a diet is simple and nutritious; it gives adequate energy and is easily digested. It is wholesome and non-toxic. It affords immense variety, and is also pleasing to the eye and palate. *Sattvic* foods are palatable, savoury, sweet, juicy and health-giving. They are agreeable to the taste, too. These are foods such as wheat, rice, green beans, dairy products, fruits, vegetables, etc.

We must eat *sattvic* food, for it purifies heart, mind and body. Man is what he eats, according to a German proverb. The mind is also a product of the food you eat. So, you must be careful! Before you begin to eat, mentally offer your food as an *ahuti* to the Lord: then your food will give you strength for work and service. Also, when you are eating, make sure that the atmosphere around you is peaceful. Do not eat in the midst of noises.

In the Gita, Sri Krishna urges Arjuna to adhere to a *sattvic* diet.

Sattvic food not merely appeals to the tongue, it is a source of nutrition to mind and body. Naturally, vegetarian foods such as fruits, milk, nuts, lentils and vegetables are the best kind of *sattvic* food.

Let me hasten to add, men and women of *sattva* are not confined to India! In the West too, as Gurudev Sadhu Vaswani pointed out, there are very many scholars of *sattvic* temperament, but their concern is less with Eternity than with the future and the present: they are concerned with plans and programmes of reform and progress.

In India, even after centuries of anglicization and

recent trends of globalisation, we have not forgotten that the goal of life is enlightenment, *mukti*, emancipation from bondage. This is why we still find men, even in middle life, who give up position and power, wealth and academic pursuit, to become *jignasus*, seekers after enlightenment, seekers after God. Their endeavour is to transcend material life to a life of contemplation and one-pointed devotion to the Divine Reality. This aspiration for the life beyond, this desire for Liberation is present in the heart of several men and women of India, even when they are leading their busy, stressful worldly lives. Perhaps this is why India still remains the nation with the largest vegetarian population.

Vegetarianism and Religion

Although vegetarianism is associated most strongly with the Indian religious traditions, especially Hinduism and Jainism, there are several subsects among the Western religions, with committed minority groups that actively promote and propagate vegetarian or even vegan lifestyles.

Hinduism:

The Hindu way of life is certainly one of the prominent factors that prompt people to take to vegetarianism. Although many Hindus are not 'pure' vegetarians, at least 20% practise vegetarianism strictly. It is safe to say that almost all Hindus avoid beef, as the cow is held in veneration. Many Hindus also abstain from all forms of flesh food during certain special days like *Chathurthi, Ekadashi,* certain days of the week, and more especially during the month of *Shravan* (August-September). In general, Hindu vegetarians consume milk and dairy products; but they avoid eggs. In fact, milk, butter, clarified butter and curds are considered to be wholesome parts of a traditional Hindu diet.

The ancient Hindu scriptures advocate a vegetarian diet. Thus for example, the *Yajur Veda* tells us: "You must not use your God given body for killing God's creatures, whether they be human, animals, or whatever." (12.32) Mahatma Gandhi, as we know, made vegetarianism his choice of lifestyle, going so far as to say, "The greatness of a nation and its moral progress can be measured by the way in which its animals are treated."

Many Hindus, especially Vaishnavites follow the practice of *naivedya*, or offering the food to the Lord before they partake of the same as *prasad*. This entails offering 'pure' food, which is equated with vegetarian food.

The Hindu law of *Karma* also acts as a strong deterrent to killing, injuring or exploiting animals: causing injury and suffering to innocent creatures is to invite the same treatment to oneself, if not now, then definitely in the reincarnations of the future. The law of *karma*, stated simply is the law of the seed: as you sow, so you reap. For those with a scientific bent of mind, it is echoed by Newton's Third Law: For every action, there is an equal and opposite reaction. If we cause bloodshed, violence and pain to innocent animals, the law states that this will be brought back on our own heads sooner or later. The case for this *karmic* reprisal is perhaps best stated in William Blake's poem, "Auguries of Innocence".

Each outcry of the hunted hare
A fibre from the brain does tear.
A skylark wounded in the wing,

A Cherubim does cease to sing.

The game cock clipp'd and arm'd for fight

Does the rising Sun affright...

Isaac Bashevis Singer, the Polish Jewish-American Nobel Laureate, asks us in a similar vein: "How can we pray to God for mercy if we ourselves have no mercy? How can we speak of rights and justice if we take an innocent creature and shed its blood?" He also goes on to say, "I personally believe that as long as human beings will go shedding the blood of animals, there will never be any peace."

Jainism:

A vegetarian diet is mandated for all Jains; in fact, they might be said to be the one community that is 100% vegetarian. *Ahimsa* (nonviolence), *aparigraha* (non-acquision), *asteya* (respect for other's rights) and *satya* (truth) are concepts that are central to Jain belief.

For Jains, *ahimsa* is the most essential religious duty; and the saying, *ahimsa paramo dharma,* is found to be inscribed in most Jain temples. Jains believe that the practise of *ahimsa* is an indispensable condition for liberation from the cycle of reincarnation, which is the ultimate goal of all Jain activities. Of course, Jains share this goal with Hindus and Buddhists, but it must be said that they are far more scrupulous, rigorous and comprehensive in applying this ideal to deeds of daily life.

As a practice, they go out of their way so as not

to hurt even small insects and other tiny animals; for them, harm caused by unintentional carelessness is as reprehensible as harm caused by deliberate action. Hence they take great pains to make sure that no minuscule animals are injured by the preparation of their meals and in the process of eating and drinking. Their scrupulous and thorough way of applying nonviolence to everyday activities, and especially to food, is a significant hallmark of Jain identity.

Pious Jains do not consume even root vegetables like potatoes and onions, as this involves pulling out the roots of the plant. Strict Jains take the *anastamita* or *anthai* vow; i.e. they do not eat after sunset, for fear of attracting small flies or insects towards the lamplight or cooking fire. They also avoid fermented food and food that has been left or stored overnight for fear of increasing its microbial content, and the destruction of more organisms.

Many prominent business houses in India owned by Jain entrepreneurs do not permit flesh food in their factories and offices.

Many predominantly Jain housing societies have also campaigned successfully to shift non vegetarian restaurants and fast food outlets out of their localities.

Buddhism:

Ahimsa is also central to Buddhist teachings: but although certain *sutras* of *Mahayana* expressly forbid the eating of meat, many Buddhists adopt different attitudes to meat-eating. It is thought that roughly 50% of Buddhists all over the world are vegetarians.

Judaism:

Although Judaism does not advocate vegetarian food, some prominent Rabbis have promoted vegetarian lifestyle, among them David Cohen and Chief Rabbi of Israel Shlomo Goren. Rabbi Isaac ha-Levi Herzog is quoted as saying: "Jews will move increasingly to vegetarianism out of their own deepening knowledge of what their tradition commands... A whole galaxy of central rabbinic and spiritual leaders...has been affirming vegetarianism as the ultimate meaning of Jewish moral teaching. Man ideally should not eat meat, for to eat meat a life must be taken, an animal must be put to death."

Taoism:

According to the Vegetarian Congress, the Chinese religion of Taoism holds nature as sacred, and this view also favours vegetarianism. Taoism teaches that *yin* and *yang* are the two fundamental energies in the world, and Taoists have always "taken the accomplishments of *yin* [the non-violent, non-aggressive approach] and rescue of creatures as their priority." (*Journal of the Academy of religion,* 54: no. 1, 1987) For example, the famous Taoist Master Li Han-Kung explicitly prohibited "those who consume meat" from his holy mountain. Taoist simplicity encourages eating vegetables, grains, and fruits instead of meat. According to the Tao, the process of meat production tends to be too *yang*, too aggressive; it involves extreme and unnecessary impact on the environment.

Christianity:

Several Christian groups, notably the Seventh Day Adventists and the Christian Vegetarian Congress take a literal interpretation of the Book of Genesis:

> And God said, "Behold, I have given you every herb bearing seed which is upon the face of all the earth, and every tree in which is the fruit of a tree yielding seed; to you it shall be for meat.
>
> And to every beast of the earth, and to every fowl of the air, and to every thing that creepeth upon the earth wherein there is life, I have given every green herb for meat"; and it was so.
>
> And God saw every thing that He had made, and behold, it was very good.
>
> Genesis 1: 29-31

There are several committed vegans and vegetarians in America and Britain who promote vegetarianism as the preferred lifestyle for Christians, based on the above lines. In fact they even go so far as to argue that it was only in the fallen state that man began to consume flesh food, for in the paradisal innocence of the Garden of Eden, there had been no violence, no killing even among animals. Christian vegetarians even claim that Christ ate a vegetarian diet. They point to the constant theme of compassion and mercy in his teachings as evidence of this claim. Early saints like St. Augustine and St. David were also vegetarians, although this might have been due to their ascetic lifestyles. St. Francis of Asissi was also a known lover of animals and birds. It is thought that a small group called the Bible Christians were the first to establish Vegetarian Group in England in the Nineteenth Century. Veganism, fasting and avoidance of flesh food in periods like Lent are more common in Eastern Christianity.

The Seventh-day Adventist Church is a Christian denomination that recommends vegetarianism as a holistic lifestyle choice to its followers. The Founders of the Seventh-day Adventist Church, including Joseph Bates and Ellen White adopted the vegetarian diet during the nineteenth century. It is said that Ellen White perceived mystic visions regarding the health benefits of the vegetarian diet. In recent years, members of the Seventh-day Adventist Church in California have been involved in research into longevity based on their own healthy lifestyle, which includes a vegetarian diet. This research has also been published in an article in

National Geographic.

In recent times, Christians who have made it their life's mission to minister to poor and hungry people, are beginning to express concern over the skewed economics of meat-production and consumption. They point out that in the United States alone 66% of the grains produced are fed to animals being raised for slaughter, wasting most grains' calories and proteins. Thus Ron Sider, a spokesman for the Eastern Baptist Theological Seminary has observed, "It is because of the high level of meat consumption that the rich minority of the world devours such an unfair share of the world's available food." (*Rich Christians in an Age of Hunger*).

Islam:

The choice to be a vegetarian is purely a personal decision in Islam. As the Islamic observances of Eid involve animal sacrifice, many Muslims believe that vegetarian diet is against the spirit of their faith. Islam forbids the consumption of certain types of meat like pork. But many minor Islamic groups and Sufi Muslims advocate a vegetarian lifestyle. Hâfiz Nazr Ahmad, a committed vegetarian by choice, argues that nowhere in the Prophet's teachings is vegetarian food proscribed to the faithful. In January 1996, The International Vegetarian Union announced the formation of the Muslim Vegetarian/Vegan Society. Islamic vegetarians quote the following verse from the *Koran* to substantiate their belief:

> There is not an animal on the earth nor a flying creature flying on two wings but they are peoples like unto you.
>
> – Koran surah 6 verse 38

Many Muslims choose vegetarian options in a meal if *halal* meat is not available.

I leave the last word on the subject of Religion and Vegetarianism to the anonymous writer whose comment from *Animal Rights Online* was sent to me by a friend:

> Vegetarians of all religions in some ways have more in common with each other than with non-vegetarians of their faith. Whether for purity of diet, compassion toward animals, creation of greater food yield per acre, environmental protection, health, aesthetics, energy conservation, religious beliefs or other, there are a growing number of vegetarian adherents in all faiths, while no faith has enough!

I say Amen to those sentiments! I also feel that in an age when the tendency is to yield to the demands of the palate, I need to express my admiration to all the brothers and sisters of all faiths, who have chosen to stay or become vegetarian on principle!

✦ *Food for Thought* ✦

Boston Vegetarian Festival Charms Taste Buds

The 16th annual Boston Vegetarian Food Festival this weekend drew vegans and omnivores alike.

On Saturday and Sunday, the 16th annual Boston Vegetarian Food Festival, presented by the Boston Vegetarian Society, served up meat free plates that satisfied the tastes of vegans and omnivores alike. Hosted at Roxbury Community College's Reggie Lewis Track and Athletic Center, the festival was comprised of dozens of booths from local and national vendors. From sprouts to Thai food to truly decadent desserts, the fair offered a spread capable of pleasing just about anyone.

Chris Allison, a member of the festival's organising committee, explained that the festival offered a way for vegetarians, vegans and curious omnivores to connect and explore vegetarianism in an environment free of both meat and pontification. Speakers on vegetarian related topics and chefs offering live cooking demonstrations aided that educational process.

"There's such a great world of options out there for anyone who wants to be vegetarian or vegan, but a lot of the world doesn't know about it, said Allison. "You think going vegetarian means eating soy-based fake meat all the time, but there are so many fantastic options out there nowadays."

"I'm a volunteer at Palomar Hospital and seeing what patients endure due to neglecting their health has turned me into a moderate health freak. Eating meat leads to higher cholesterol, which leads to higher risk of cardiovascular problems. Especially in America, our meat really isn't taken care of, so the meat here may be loaded with drugs and bad chemicals. As much as cruelty occurs to the animals, that's not my reason for being vegetarian. I just care about my health," school senior Luchie Glorio so said.

– Tufts Daily - October 31, 2011

Dessert

How to Have a Long, Healthy Life

A woman walked up to a wrinkled, bent, little old man rocking in a chair on his porch.

"I couldn't help noticing how happy you look," she said. "What's your secret for a long happy life?"

"I eat no vegetables at all, only red meat; I smoke three packs of cigarettes a day; I also drink a case of whiskey a week, binge on foods with poly unsaturated fats, and never exercise."

"That's amazing," said the woman, "how old are you?"

"Twenty-six."

CHAPTER SEVEN

VEGETARIANISM: NUTRITION FACTS

Naivedya:

He who offereth to me with devotion a leaf, a flower, a fruit, or water, that gift of love I accept, as offering of the pure heart.

– Bhagavad Gita, Ch IX, 26

Invocation:

Vegetables are Mother Nature's marvelous products. Her divine garden truly presents a blaze of brilliant colours. You can effortlessly put together a balanced diet just by choosing a bit of each colour.

– J.P. Vaswani

Apertif:

Oh, my fellow men, do not defile your bodies with sinful foods. We have corn, we have apples bending down the branches with their weight, and grapes swelling on the vines. There are sweet-flavoured herbs, and vegetables which can be cooked and softened over the fire, nor are you denied milk or thyme-scented honey. The earth affords a lavish supply of riches, of innocent foods, and offers you banquets that involve no bloodshed or slaughter; only beasts satisfy their hunger with flesh, and not even all of those, because horses, cattle, and sheep live on grass.

– Pythagoras

✦ Starters ✦

In his book, *Why You Don't Need Meat*, Peter Cox tells us that millions upon billions of dollars are spent on advertising by the meat industry in affluent countries. This is intensive, high-pressure advertising; what is called 'saturation coverage'. The sort you and your children cannot escape from...

All that money, Cox warns us, is spent only with one objective: to ensure that their consumers keep on buying meat and meat products. They can't afford to let people stop! They can't even afford to allow people to cut back on the quantity they buy.

They can afford to spend all that money because the size of the meat industry is absolutely staggering! When it is all added up, it is worth billions upon billions of dollars a year. In comparison, the millions they spend on advertising is small – almost chicken feed!

✦ Main Course ✦

Let me repeat this. In practical terms food can be of two categories: food of violence or *himsa* – food that includes fish, flesh and fowl; the alternative is the food of *ahimsa* or non-violence, in other words, a vegetarian diet. During the last fifty years or more, medical experts and nutritionists have largely inclined to the opinion that a vegetarian diet is the best option for good health.

As we have seen earlier, anatomical and physiological studies point to the fact that civilised, evolved man is meant to be a vegetarian. His entire digestive system, including his teeth, his stomach and his intestines are so structured as to prove that even nature meant him to be a vegetarian.

A vegetarian diet includes all of the following – grains such as rice, wheat, maize, millets, etc; pulses such as *dals* and lentils (beans as they are called in the west); roots and tubers like potatoes, carrots and onions; fresh and dry fruits, like apples, mango, watermelon, banana, as well as almonds, cashews, peanuts, etc; and the abundant and plentiful supply of fresh, green, leafy and non-leafy vegetables that God has blessed the earth with!

There are some people who claim that milk is an animal product and therefore should not be included in a strictly vegetarian diet. But the fact remains, that we do not kill a cow to obtain its milk.

Mahatma Gandhi who was at first an ardent advocate of a vegan diet, one which did not include milk, excluded milk totally from his diet for about six years or so. Then in 1917, he fell ill, and in his own words, "was reduced to a skeleton". The doctors warned him that he would not be able to build up enough strength to leave his bed, if milk and milk products were not included in his diet. However, Gandhiji had made a vow that he would not take milk. A doctor then suggested to him that when he had made the vow, he could only have had in mind the milk of the cow and the buffalo, so the vow should not prevent him from taking goat's milk! That was how Gandhiji began to take goat's milk. At that time, he himself admitted, it seemed to bring him new life! He picked up rapidly and was soon able to leave his sick bed. "On account of this and several similar experiences," he writes, "I have been forced to admit the necessity of adding milk to the strict vegetarian diet."

At that time, Gandhiji wrote prophetically: "I am convinced that in the vast vegetable kingdom there must be some kind, which, while supplying those necessary substances which we derive from milk, is free from its ethical drawbacks.

Nutrition experts now feel that soya milk and tofu can indeed provide such an alternative.

Why Choose Vegetarian?

The arguments in favour of a vegetarian diet fall under three categories:

1. Physiological: Flesh diet is held to be responsible for serious diseases such as cancer.

2. Moral and ethical: There is much to be said against the wanton cruelty inflicted upon dumb and defenceless animals.

3. Economic: It has been proved that equal or better nutrition can be obtained from vegetable foods more efficiently and economically than from flesh foods.

However, we are now looking at a vegetarian diet in relation to the maintenance of good health in human beings. Millions of individuals all over the world subsist entirely on a vegetarian diet; and they have remained in good health and led very productive lives. Therefore, it is time we became aware of some basic nutrition facts about vegetarian food. Some of the nutrition facts I mention below are well known; others, I have gathered from my own reading as well as from conversations with experts in the field and like-minded brothers and sisters.

Proteins

What are proteins? How much protein do we need?

People who do not know the answer to these basic questions, still persist in the belief that meat is the only source of protein available to man. They justify their flesh diet as the only one that satisfies our necessity for protein.

Proteins, according to experts, are long collections of amino acids constructed from carbon, hydrogen, oxygen and nitrogen. Next to water, protein is the most plentiful substance in the human body. It helps build muscles, blood, hair, skin and nails as well as our internal organs. It helps us to produce various enzymes, antibodies and hormones.

The amount of protein we need depends on the individual - taking into account factors like height, weight and level of activity.

Indeed, meat has been mistakenly identified with protein in the minds of many mothers. But, it has been amply demonstrated that sufficient protein can be obtained from non-animal sources such as *dals*, beans, lentils, nuts, etc. In fact, a vegetarian diet has been proven to be an excellent source of quality protein, as well as the other nutritional constituents, at a very reasonable price. For the average family, an imaginative meatless diet of salads, soups, casseroles, loaves, stews, legumes, fresh breads, and fruit and nuts, can sharply reduce the food bill, while supplying adequate quantities of protein.

It has been found too, that the maximum amount of protein is generated by combining various food groups in a diet, a practice that has been handed down from our grandmothers in vegetarian households. Thus, a good combination for protein is rice and *dal* – a staple in India. Other such combinations are:

- Milk and cereals
- Pasta and Cheese
- Minestrone Soup
- Brown rice and beans

The average minimum protein requirement of a man or woman is estimated to be around 45 gms a day. This is easily available in milk (preferably skimmed, so as to remove excess fat), curds, cheese, lentils, soya beans, peanuts and sunflower seeds. The world famous nutritionist, Earl Mindell, writes in his book, *The Vitamin Bible*: "A good rice and beans dish with some cottage cheese can be as nourishing, less expensive and lower in fat than a steak."

Iron

Iron is needed by the body to make haemoglobin, found in red blood cells, which carries oxygen to all parts of the body. It also helps to produce myoglobin in muscle cells to transport oxygen in the muscles. Lack of iron is a very common nutritional deficiency, especially among women. This is as true of western countries as of the third world. The cause is a poor basic diet, with over consumption of refined foods. It is commonly thought that a vegetarian diet is low in iron. This is not true. Vegetarian foods rich in iron include spinach and green leafy vegetables, beet root, black beans, cashews, hempseed, kidney beans, lentils, oatmeal, raisins, black-eyed peas, soybeans, many breakfast cereals, sunflower seeds, chickpeas, tomato juice, tempeh, molasses, and whole-wheat bread. Vegan diets can often be higher in iron than vegetarian diets, because dairy products are low in iron.

Calcium

Calcium, as many of us know, is essential for healthy bones and teeth. Junk food that is fancied by many young people is one of the main reasons of calcium deficiency. Meat is not a good source of calcium. The calcium we need is obtained from foods like milk, cheese, seaweed, spinach, molasses, chickpeas, almonds and raisins.

Vitamin A

Vitamin A is actually formed in the healthy human body with the help of carotene, the substance that gives yellow colouring to certain fruits and vegetables. It is stored in our livers and used for cell formation as well as to aid night vision. Fruits and vegetables of yellow colour (pumpkin, carrots, papaya, melons, and peaches) are good sources of Vitamin A.

It is also found in mustard greens (*sarso*), tomatoes and green peppers. The spice paprika, commonly used in India is also a well known source.

The B Group Vitamins

These are vital to our well being, and all of us must ensure that we know where to find them and include them in our diet. B1, B6, B12 and other vitamins are all rather different from each other; but they have a lot in common too.

1. They are all water soluble
2. They pass through the body very quickly.
3. We need a regular source of them in our daily diet.
4. They occur naturally in yeast and yeast products.
5. We need them to convert the carbohydrates in our food to usable energy.
6. They help the nervous system to function properly.
7. We need more of them during periods of stress, high activity, or infection.

Contrary to the propaganda put out by the meat industry, flesh foods are not the only sources of B Vitamins.

B1 (Thiamin) is found in millets, wheat germ, dried peas and sunflower seeds.

B2 (Riboflavin) is found in broccoli, almonds, skimmed milk, avocado and yeast.

B6 (Pyridoxine) is found in whole grains, brewer's yeast, peanuts, raisins, orange/tomato juice, as well as bananas.

B12 (Cobalamine) does not occur normally in plant foods. Needed for cell division and blood formation, it is important for the efficient functioning of the brain and the nervous system. It is also related to fatty acid synthesis and energy production. Animals absorb this vitamin from bacteria. Its requirement for the body is very minimal, but vital. It can be obtained from dairy products, fortified cereals, soya products and yeast supplements.

Folic acid, as the name suggests (foliage) is abundant in green leafy vegetables, but not commonly found in meat. As it is destroyed by cooking, fresh green leafy vegetables are recommended by nutritionists.

Vitamin C

This vitamin promotes the formation of connective tissues, and thus plays an important role in the healing of wounds as well as in the continuous regeneration of the body. It fights bacterial infections and helps to keep bones and teeth strong. Vitamin C is sensitive both to heat and light, so we cannot really look for it in cooked foods. As it is well preserved in an acidic environment citrus fruits are an excellent source for this vitamin. Your daily glass of freshly squeezed orange juice is enough to give you the required dosage. Other rich sources are gooseberries (*amla*), black currants, berries, red and green peppers, sprouted beans, green leafy vegetables and tomatoes.

Vitamin D

This is called the 'sunshine vitamin' because that is where most of us get it! The sun's rays act on a fatty substance present in our skin and convert it into Vitamin D. Low levels of vitamin D have often been associated with osteoporosis, hypertension and diabetes. Butter, margarine, whole milk and vegetable oil are other sources of this vitamin.

Vitamin E

This vitamin is described as nature's most powerful anti-oxidant. Antioxidants boost the immune system and can help prevent cancer, heart disease and many other forms of major illness. They also slow down the effects of ageing and can fend off conditions like Alzheimer's. This vitamin is not found to any appreciable extent in meat or meat products. The main sources are nuts, sunflower seeds and cold pressed vegetable oils.

Vitamin K

The newest vitamin was identified by a Danish Scientist in the 1920s. It is essential for blood coagulation. It is found in cabbage, kale, kelp, mustard greens, spinach, Brussels sprouts, seaweed, molasses, green leafy vegetables and olive oil. Fruits such as avocado, kiwifruit and grapes are also high in vitamin K. Surprisingly, we are told by nutritionists that two tablespoons of parsley contain 153% of the recommended daily amount of vitamin K!

Healthy fats

Fats – sounds like something we should not eat! But fats play an important part in our diet. They are vital for the development of the brain and the nervous system in children; that is why children are encouraged to drink whole milk, while the rest of us stick to low fat or skimmed milk. Fat is a rich source of calories, and that is why we need to watch our intake of oil and butter. Fat is also needed to carry and store essential fat-soluble vitamins, like vitamins A and D.

When we eat a lot of high fat foods, we not only consume a lot of calories; we also put on unnecessary weight. Eating too much fat also increases the risk of getting diseases like cancer, heart disease, high blood pressure or stroke. Health experts recommend that we should get no more than 30% of our calories from fat to reduce our risk of getting these diseases.

If there is one thing that people have come to fear as much as a nuclear explosion, it is that dreaded substance called cholesterol. Increased level of cholesterol in the blood is responsible for coronary heart disease and also gall-stones. It is now a well-known fact that animal fats raise the cholesterol level in the blood. Further, the saturated fatty acids in animal fat, aggravate coronary heart disease.

Cholesterol is actually a steroid present in all animal cells. It occurs in almost all foods of animal origin, such as meat, fish, milk, cream, cheese, eggs and butter. Cholesterol is present in the fat portion of these foods. Most foods of plant origin, such as fruits, vegetables, cereals, do not contain cholesterol.

Research has proved that animal fats raise the cholesterol level of the blood, while certain vegetables actually lower it.

Saturated fats are the only fatty acids that raise blood cholesterol levels. They are found in meats and whole dairy products like milk, cheese, cream and ice cream. Some saturated fats are also found in plant foods like tropical oils (coconut or palm kernel oil). Butter, margarine, and fats in meat and dairy products are all especially high in saturated fat.

Unsaturated fats are usually liquid at room temperature. They are found in most vegetable products and oils. Using foods containing "polyunsaturated" and "mono unsaturated" fats does not increase our risk of heart disease. However, we would do well to remember that like all other fats, unsaturated fats also give us calories for every gram. So eating too much of these types of fat may also make us gain weight.

Trans fats are produced when liquid oil is made into a solid fat. This process is called hydrogenation. Trans fats act like saturated fats and can raise your cholesterol level. The foods to avoid in this category are junk foods such as crisps, wafers, processed foods, high fat baked goods and cookies.

Another factor we must consider in evaluating the health aspects of a non-vegetarian diet is this: the amount of toxic wastes present in the flesh of a dead animal are very high. Thus, when we eat the flesh of animals, we are not only consuming the so-called nutritive portions, but also these poisonous waste-products. It is not possible for the body to eliminate these poisons immediately and effectively.

If after all this information, some people still continue to worry about whether a vegetarian diet can provide all essential nutrients, let me assure them, with the backing of the best nutritionists: it is very easy to have a well-balanced diet with vegetarian foods, since these foods provide plenty of protein. Careful combining of foods is not difficult. Any normal variety of vegetarian foods provides more than enough protein for the body's needs. If at all there is somewhat less protein in a vegetarian diet than a meat-eater's diet, this is actually an advantage. Excess protein has been linked to kidney stones, osteoporosis, and possibly heart disease and some cancers. A diet focused on beans, whole grains, and vegetables contains adequate amounts of protein without the "overdose" most meat-eaters get. Nor are highly processed 'meat substitutes' a must. Rather, what we need is a revaluation of the ways we choose and prepare our traditional, natural foods. Make sure you put enough colours, flavours and textures of wholesome vegetarian foods on your plate. Your diet will then take care of itself!

✦ *Food for Thought* ✦

A balanced vegetarian diet is low in fat (especially saturated fat), high in complex carbohydrates and packed with a variety of fruits and vegetables; just as the government and the medical profession recommend.

Research has shown that vegetarians are less likely to suffer from obesity, coronary heart disease, high blood pressure, type II diabetes, some diet-related cancers, diverticular disease, appendicitis, constipation and gallstones.

Vegetarians are far more likely than the general population to eat the recommended five portions of fruit and vegetables each day.

Becoming a vegetarian is easy, but everyone should think about what they eat. There are plenty of resources available by way of the internet as well as books to help you get started and to stay healthy.

"Appropriately planned vegetarian diets, including total vegetarian or vegan diet, are healthful, nutritionally adequate, and may provide health benefits in the prevention and treatment of certain diseases." [American Dietetic Association]
                                   – Vegetarian Society Pamphlet

Dessert

In the beginning, God created the Heavens and the Earth and populated the Earth with broccoli, cauliflower and spinach, green and yellow and red vegetables of all kinds, so Man and Woman would live long and healthy lives.

Then using God's great gifts, Satan created Ice Cream, and Donuts. And Satan said, "You want chocolate with that?" And Man said, "Yes!" and Woman said, "And as long as you're at it, add some sprinkles." And they gained 10 pounds. And Satan smiled.

And God created the healthful yogurt that Woman might keep the figure that Man found so fair. And Satan brought forth white refined flour from the wheat, and sugar from the cane and combined them.

And Woman went from size 6 to size 14.

So God said, "Try my fresh green salad" And Satan presented Thousand-Island Dressing with plenty of mayonaisse, chicken nuggets, sausages and garlic toast on the side. And Man and Woman unfastened their belts following the repast. God then said, "I have sent you heart healthy vegetables and olive oil in which to cook them." And Satan brought

forth deep fried fish and chicken-fried steak so big it needed its own platter.

And Man gained more weight and his cholesterol went through the roof.

God then brought forth running shoes so that His children might lose those extra pounds. And Satan gave cable TV with a remote control so Man would not have to toil changing the channels.

And Man and Woman laughed and cried before the flickering blue light and gained pounds.

Then God brought forth the potato, naturally low in fat and brimming with nutrition. And Satan peeled off the healthful skin and sliced the starchy center into chips and deep-fried them. And Man gained pounds.

God then gave delicious fruits and greens so that Man might consume fewer calories and still satisfy his appetite. And Satan created huge one pound beef burgers and double cheese burger.

Then he asked, "You want fries with that?"

And Man replied, "Yes! And super size them!" And Satan said, "It is good." And Man went into cardiac arrest.

– Nutrition joke on Twitter

CHAPTER EIGHT

VEGETARIAN DIET:

DEBUNKING A FEW MYTHS

Prejudice is one of the world's greatest labour-saving devices; it enables you to form an opinion without having to dig up the facts.

- Laurence Peter

Myths, in the sense of half-truths, falsehoods and fanciful rumours are spread about things people do not know fully about, or suspect as being contrary to their own interests and against their way of thinking. Vegetarians have been a much maligned dietary minority in this regard. In this section, I would like to debunk certain myths and theories that have been spread about vegetarianism and vegetarians. These myths and the debunking arguments have been shared with me by young, enthusiastic 'Veg lovers'.

1. All vegetarians are weirdos.

I do not mind repeating this again and again: vegetarians are not freaks, eccentrics or ascetics in hair shirts! A vegetarian is a completely normal person with completely normal food cravings, someone who has a broad range of friends, enjoys a good time, reads and listens to music, and so on. All he chooses is the option of not eating anything that was once alive and had eyes to see! As a diehard vegetarian puts it: "Now remove from this normal average person's diet anything that once had eyes, and, wham!, you have yourself a vegetarian".

A vegetarian diet is just a sensible food option among many. What is so weird about the choice of foods you want to eat? Many people are now becoming open minded about a vegetarian diet and also willing to discuss it with friends and nutritionists. As for being weirdos – whom exactly did you have in mind? Mahatma Gandhi?

Bernard Shaw? And for the younger generation, star idols like Brad Pitt and Kim Basinger? Need I add more names? And do remember, Hitler was NOT a vegetarian, whatever the myth-makers may say.

2. **Vegetarians are week, sickly and malnourished.**

   Like their fellow human beings, vegetarians come in all shapes and sizes. Many famous sports persons, including cricketers like Kris Srikanth, R. Ashwin and Murali Karthik are vegetarians.

3. **It is very difficult to be a vegetarian in UK or USA.**

   Not at all! Vegetarian foods are now freely available in supermarkets all over the world, and many customer friendly restaurants are ready to go out of their way to serve the most fastidious diners with their choice of food.

4. **Vegetarians are just hypocritical. They are all so concerned about cruelty to animals, but continue to use leather shoes and wear silks.**

   Vegetarians are what they want to be, it is a personal choice they have made. Few vegetarians I know climb the high moral ground to proclaim to the rest of the world that they are superior. On the other hand, they are in a minority that often gets teased and slighted. As for leather and silk, I know that people who are sensitive to the issues of animal cruelty, will not choose leather or silk, after all, there are very good substitutes available for both!

5. **All vegetarians are militant animal rights activists.**

Not true! There are many people who are switching over to a vegetarian diet purely on health grounds. Many vegetarians appreciate the efforts being made by animal rights activists, and empathise with animal suffering. But not all of them take to the streets or adopt militancy to fight the cause. It's the same as environmental ethics – thousands of people avoid using plastic bags and consciously segregate garbage. But they do not go on protests or rallies.

6. **A Vegetarian diet does not provide enough protein/calcium/iron/vitamins.**

Do read the chapters on health benefits and nutrition facts where these issues have been discussed. A balanced vegetarian diet provides all the nutrients necessary for the human body.

7. **Humans were meant to eat flesh food. God created animals for human consumption.**

Human anatomy suggests otherwise! And if you believe that animals are 'resources' for human exploitation, remember: the nineteenth century threw out a similar view about slaves as free labour resources; the twentieth century threw out the pernicious view of women as goods and chattels; and I firmly believe that the present century will accord a similar status to animals as creatures with the right to live for themselves!

8. **Vegetarians are people who have given up indulgences like good appetising food.**

   Vegetarians are normal people with normal food cravings, who love good food and enjoy tasty delicacies!

   And they are hardly starved for choice when they are at home. Nowadays, good restaurants are also ready to serve them wholesome and appetising fare.

9. **A vegetarian diet is at best a health compromise.**

   It is flesh food eaters who are choosing unhealthy animal products which are actually compromising their health!

   Misleading claims by the meat industry hold up the erroneous claim that a vegetarian diet is insufficient and nutritionally lacking. A poorly planned, ill-balanced diet may be a compromise, whether it is vegetarian or otherwise. (e.g. a plateful of French fries and fried chicken, or a plateful of ice cream or a double beef burger or even a bowlful of uncooked spinach). Most nutritionists and doctors will agree when I say that human beings flourish when eating a well planned plant-based diet.

10. Vegetarians think that animals are better than other human beings.

No! Vegetarians recognise that animals are sentient beings, and respect their right to live. Their aim is to cause minimal pain or suffering to all creatures and to avoid all killing in the name of food and nutrition.

CHAPTER NINE

VEGETARIANISM FAQS

1. How many vegetarians are there in the world today?

It is hard to get exact figures, but let me share with you what I have read. The 2008, "Vegetarianism in America" study published by the *Vegetarian Times* Magazine, puts the number of U.S. adult vegetarians at 7.3 million, or 3.2 percent of the population. In England, vegetarianism got a huge boost from the mad cow scare. According to a 2006 Mintel survey, 6 percent of the population, or 3.6 million people, are vegetarians, and 10 percent eat no red meat. This probably makes the UK the European country with the largest proportion of its population that is vegetarian. Roughly 0.5 - 3% of populations are vegetarian in other European countries.

A study done by the Israeli Ministry of Health claims 8.5 percent of the Israeli population, or 595,000 people, are vegetarian, which is an impressive figure.

India holds more vegetarians than the rest of the world combined. A 2006 survey by *The Hindu* newspaper estimated that roughly 40 percent of the population, or 399 million people, are vegetarians. Other estimates cite a lesser percentage.

2. **What are the different types of vegetarians?**

    I can refer to three broad categories: 1. Vegetarians do not eat meat, poultry, eggs or fish. Dairy products like milk, butter and yoghurt are acceptable to them. 2. Vegans exclude milk, milk products as well as eggs from their food. 3. Lacto-ovo vegetarians eat eggs and drink milk. Most Hindus and Jains are lacto-vegetarians: they consume milk as well as milk products.

3. **Why on earth do people take to a vegetarian diet? In a state of ignorance perhaps?**

    That is making a mockery of people whose families and entire communities have been vegetarian for generations!

    There is such a thing as courage of conviction, faith in your religious and cultural traditions and standing up for your principles! As for new converts to vegetarianism, they usually give up meat for a variety of ethical, environmental, and health reasons.

4. **I think vegetarianism is a personal choice to be made by the individual. Why do societies and associations and spiritual leaders like you wish to advocate this cause?**

    Practising and advocating good principles is not wrong! When we know something is good, we tend to share it with others so that all may benefit from the same. So is it with vegetarianism. We believe it can only be in the best interests of all humanity and all of creation if more and more people turn vegetarian. So we promote and propagate the cause we believe in. Most of us do not believe in coercion or compulsion.

5. **Can an athlete receive adequate nutrition from a vegetarian diet?**

India has produced many athletes and cricketers who are vegetarians. The US and Europe too, have athletes who are committed vegetarians.

6. **Why are some cheeses, jellies and custards labeled vegetarian, while others are not?**

Unknown to many of us, food processes sometimes involve substances of animal origin which we do not normally associate with or expect to find in a particular category of food. Thus, to most of us cheese is a milk product; jelly is a sweetened dessert. Cheese is made by coagulating milk to give curds which are then separated from the liquid (whey). The solids are then processed and matured to produce a wide variety of cheeses. Milk is usually coagulated by the addition of rennet. The active ingredient of rennet is the enzyme, chymosin (also known as rennin). The usual source of rennet is the stomach of slaughtered newly-born calves.

This is why many strict vegetarians generally avoid commercial brands of cheese.

However, we now have several varieties of vegetarian cheese available in the market. These are manufactured using rennet from either fungal or lacto-bacterial sources.

Similarly, jelly is made with the use of gelatine which is made from meat collagen found in the hooves of calves and other animals. But jelly manufacturers have now started using a variety of vegetable origin substances to substitute this: they include various vegetable tree gums, plant extracts as well as seaweeds like agar agar. Eggless cakes and custards are also readily available in supermarkets now. All a vegetarian has to do is to read labels carefully.

7. **Have you any idea of the number of animals slaughtered for food every day?**

Such statistics are not easy to obtain. But according to 2009 documents, 59 billion animals died to feed Americans in 2009. Over a lifetime, this amounts to 15,000 animals per meat eater in the US alone.

According to FAO statistics, about 53 billion land animals are slaughtered annually worldwide in other countries. (It should be noted that at the time the numbers were compiled, they were the minimum numbers of animals killed each year. The actual numbers may be significantly greater in so far as some countries or territories either did not report, or deliberately excluded, some statistics.)

8. Can domestic pets like cats and dogs be vegetarian? Is a vegetarian diet cruel to them?

Cats and dogs are not herbivores by nature. But having said that, they are not likely to come to any harm from a vegetarian diet! Enlightened pet owners always take advice from their vets regarding supplements. (Although I have known a lot of vegetarian households which would not dream of giving their pets anything that they would not eat themselves, cats for one do go out after their own choice of fare!)

9. I love cakes! Can they be made well without eggs? Will they taste the same?

Eggless cakes are popular and easy to make! In cake making, eggs are used to make them light and fluffy.

Tofu, soya flower, corn starch, bananas or even commercial egg substitutes may be used, depending on the need. About 70% of the calories in eggs are from fat. Much of this fat is saturated. Eggs are also high in cholesterol. Therefore smart cooks do without them!

10. Didn't God create animals to be food for men?

Many people use this claim as a justification for meat consumption. I beg to differ. The Bible, for instance, is used to support claims that God gave man 'dominion' over the animals to do with them as they please. As for man, he has pleased himself with animals by killing them indiscriminately, mostly for being a source of food and also just for fun, like fox hunting, etc.

My conception of God differs slightly. He put the same spark of life into every one of his creatures. Animals are sentient beings and feel the pain and agony of being killed even as humans do! In my opinion, God expects us, as human beings, to love and care for animals and birds, who, as Gurudev Sadhu Vaswani said, are our younger brothers and sisters in the One family of Creation.

11. It is expensive to be a vegetarian, isn't it?

On the contrary, it is much less expensive to eat a vegetarian diet! You are probably thinking of delicatessens or expensive organic food shops! Most of the staples of a vegetarian diet are cheaper than meat and meat products. Rice, wheat, beans, lentils and vegetables are any day less expensive than fish, poultry, meat and eggs. And remember too, it is not easy to calculate the cost of all the medical expenses saved by staying healthy on a vegetarian diet!

Vegetarianism could extend your life by several years, as well as lower your risk of heart disease, cancer and dementia. It is better for the planet, reducing water usage and global-warming gases. (And it certainly improves the health of the cow or pig or lamb or chicken that you would have otherwise devoured.)

12. **I think a vegetarian diet day after day must be quite boring. Do you agree?**

A vegetarian diet is simple and nutritious; it gives adequate energy and is easily digested. It is wholesome and nontoxic. It affords immense variety, and is also pleasing to the eye and palate. Fruits have been described as the food of the Gods – and also the food of the *rishis* and *yogis*. They are nature's own special delicacies, brought to luscious goodness in the warmth of the sun. They are rich in vitamins and minerals, and also give us plenty of fibre. Vegetables are Mother Nature's marvellous products. Her divine garden truly presents a blaze of brilliant colours with the red and yellow, green and purple, pink, white, brown and mauve of these delicious wonders!

A vegetarian connoisseur will be proud to tell you that you can effortlessly put together a balanced diet just by choosing a bit of each colour! A balanced mix of leafy vegetables, 'seed' vegetables and pulses produces a perfect combination in terms of nutrition and energy. Salads are surely everyone's favourite!

13. What about eating out?

I understand from friends that there are several restaurants all over the world that pay special attention to the diet preferences of their clientele. But I also know that many vegetarian friends in India prefer to eat out at vegetarian restaurants, for fear of foods getting mixed up by careless handling.

14. How can I get started on a vegetarian diet?

If you are not a 'born' vegetarian, experts suggest the following steps:

1. Understand your reason for going vegetarian. Let your motives be clear to you.

2. Choose the type of vegetarianism you wish to adopt – with or without eggs, dairy products, etc.

3. Do your homework on the nutrition. Understand your own protein needs and how it may be obtained from sources other than animals.

4. Start gradually, by reducing your meat and flesh consumption. Give up meat once a week or oftener.

5. Find healthy, tasty substitutes for the foods

you are cutting out. Do not resort to junk food to satisfy your cravings.

6. Invest in a good vegetarian cookbook. Try a variety of recipes with a variety of fresh vegetables, cereals and legumes!

Many people skip these carefully planned steps and jump headlong into a vegetarian diet on a sudden emotional or ethical impulse, instant conversion, as it were. It is not that hard; it only requires a little more determination.

15. What are the changes I can expect?

Let me quote from a convert to vegetarianism: "I just kept thinking, not what am I losing, but what am I gaining: a clearer conscience and a healthier lifestyle!" Experiences do vary, but most people switching over to a vegetarian diet report a sense of lightness, and added energy levels. Many former meat eaters report a loss of weight and clearer skin. You will also note a reduction in what are called 'tummy troubles'. But above all, you will feel good about yourself! Some people report initial cravings for the foods they gave up, but if you are committed, these cravings don't persist. The satisfaction people receive from living in accordance with their principles usually more than compensates for the slight inconvenience.

16. What is a flexitarian? Can I be a semi-vegetarian?

Flexitarians are people who convert to vegetarian food for medical rather than ethical reasons. They are also known as part-time vegetarians. They are people in the middle, who often turn to meat for whatever reason.

They belong to an ever growing majority who are acutely conscious of the health benefits of avoiding meat, but are unable to make the full transition. Instead, they do their best to cut back on their meat consumption.

As for your second question, my answer can only be this: why be a semi-anything? Why do things half-heartedly?

17. Animals kill each other for food. So what is wrong if we kill them for our food?

This is the familiar excuse used by some people to justify the killing of animals for meat. Why should we be in such a hurry to descend from our evolved state as human beings to the not-so-evolved state of predators?

The goal of a thinking vegetarian is to eliminate direct, unnecessary suffering of animals at the hands of humans.

He would not find it acceptable to kill any animal to satisfy his palate. It is as simple as that!

18. **If all of us were to turn vegetarian, won't earth be overrun with cows, pigs, lambs, sheep and chickens?**

I am constantly amused by these pseudo-global concerns expressed by so many people who are reluctant to turn vegetarian! My friends told me about a book which blames agriculture rather than factory farming for destroying the environment! The worldwide explosion in the population of slaughterhouse animals is due to the unhealthy and cruel practices of factory farming. If they were to be bred naturally, we would not have such enormous numbers of meat-cattle at all. We are now using artificial methods, dangerous methods, to breed these animals. They are given growth hormones to put on more flesh and increase their weight, so that they fetch more money in the meat market. Hens and cows are treated with steroids to increase reproduction.

Once these horrors are stopped, there would be no bio-problems of the sort you fear. Nature will take care of itself! It is only when we interfere with the laws of nature, that we create problems, and the responsibility devolves on us to sort them out. Giving up meat is a humane and healthy choice. Do not complicate it by unnecessary considerations.

19. Why do people become vegetarians?

I have said this earlier: on the grounds of religious and spiritual convictions; on ethical or moral grounds; on grounds of compassion; and for environmental or ideological reasons such as animal rights and the problem of world hunger.

20. How can you claim that vegetarians are more humane?

I make no such claim! But the truth is that the food we eat affects not only our bodies but also our minds, our attitude and thinking. Mahatma Gandhi said, "There is a great deal of truth in the saying that man becomes what he eats." When you go vegetarian by choice, you have exercised your conscious option to be ethical, moral and non-violent in your diet and lifestyle. In general, vegetarians are less aggressive than their non-vegetarian counterparts, although human vices like greed, false pride and prejudice, also play an important role in making the character of man. In sum, vegetarianism, in conjunction with other virtues, does lead to our physical and mental well-being.

21. You claim that vegetarianism will lead to peace in the world. I fail to see the connection.

I firmly believe that until we grow in the vision of brotherhood, world peace can never be a reality. "May we grow in the spirit of fellowship and understanding," say our ancient Hindu scriptures. And the *Rig Veda*, perhaps the oldest of all scriptures says: "Together walk ye, and together talk ye, and together know ye your minds!"

The world, I believe is a garden of God. God is in all that is, men and women, birds and animals, fish and fowl, worms and insects, in trees and flowers, in rivers and rocks, in stones and stars, in this pen that scribbles, and even the paper on which my moving finger writes. *Krishna! Krishna! Krishna* is in all–and we all are in *Krishna!* When we have this vision of the One-in-all and All-in-one, we will grow in the spirit of Brotherhood of all creation!

My vision of fellowship and brotherhood shows me a world in which the right to life is accorded to every creature that breathes the breath of life! How can wars cease until we stop all killing? How can we claim to seek world peace when we continue to slaughter sentient creatures? For if a man kills an animal for food, he will not hesitate in killing a fellow man whom he regards as an enemy! Therefore I urge my friends, even as I urge you, dear reader, through the pages of this book, let us grow in the true spirit of brotherhood. Let us grow in the spirit of Reverence for all Life!

This, I believe is the first and vital step towards world peace.

22. How does a token Meatless Day help spread the cause of vegetarianism?

"One day at a time" is a good, easy beginning for everyone. One day is all it takes to create an awareness, to plant a seed of sensitivity in the minds of people in regard to the cruelties that are perpetrated on animals day after day.

I am told that on an average, a meat-eating human being consumes 7,500 creatures, big and small, over his lifetime.

7500 animals, every one of them who loves life as much as he who consumes them! The time has come when we must realise the moral inviolability of non-human animals.

On this one day, millions of brothers and sisters pledge to go meatless as a mark of tribute to Gurudev Sadhu Vaswani, who was the voice of the voiceless ones. On this one day, many organisations and offices go meatless.

Slaughter houses are closed in Maharashtra and other states. Is it not a worthwhile cause to save so many creatures at least on this one day?

Our Meatless Day and Animal Rights Day is a small step in that direction.

23. Can I lose weight on a vegetarian diet?

As any dietician will tell you, a vegetarian diet will help you lose weight only if you make the right choice of foods!

Research shows that adults and children who follow a vegetarian diet are generally leaner than non-vegetarians.

This is probably because a vegetarian diet typically includes less saturated fat and emphasises more fruits, vegetables, whole grains and plant-based proteins, foods that are more filling and less calorie dense.

If you eat more calories than you need, you will gain weight, whether you eat vegetarian food or otherwise.

24. You are so concerned about the suffering of animals. I ask you, don't humans deserve more sympathy than lesser creatures?

This is the specious argument often used by anti-animal rights people.

Of course people like me are sensitive to the cause of human pain and suffering! But we are also concerned that the same sympathy should be extended to our dumb and defenceless brethren who have no TV, no media and no advocates to fight for their rights!

When I ask you to treat animals with compassion and avoid cruelty in using them, I am not asking you to trample on human rights and exploit other human beings.

We tend to be speceicists, and fail to recognise the rights of other non-human creatures. We need to extend our compassion to other forms of life. That is what will prove our evolved status over the rest of creation!

25. What is wrong with free range eggs?

In the context of this book, free range eggs and free range animals also have a life, and their right to life is inviolable. Free-range eggs are produced by birds that are permitted to roam freely within a farmyard, a shed or a chicken coop. This is different from factory-farmed birds that are typically enclosed in battery cages. Similarly, free range animals are allowed to roam freely instead of being contained in any manner.

Although their conditions are far better than that of animals in factory-farming, what matters in the end is that their lives are ruthlessly destroyed to please someone's palate. This can never be acceptable to ethical vegetarians.

26. What is your view on the use of silk and wool as fabrics?

The truly compassionate people will not be

comfortable using either material!

In South India, which is famous for its Kanjivaram silks, the *Paramacharya* of Kanchi made the bold appeal to women not to wear their traditional silk sarees, on humanitarian grounds.

I am told that we are now offered *ahimsa* silk, which is extracted from discarded pupa shells of silkworms, instead of killing the worms.

Some people argue that leather is made from the carcass/skins of dead animals. I for one, would not recommend its usage, when synthetic substitutes are freely available.

27. **Most vegetarians are people who cannot afford meat, are they not? Anyone who had the choice would prefer to eat meat and eggs, surely!**

Millions of healthy individuals in the world today, have subsisted on a wholly fleshless diet, and have remained in good health, while leading long and productive lives.

Thus we have

- Innumerable Hindus, Jains, as well as some Chinese who have adhered to a vegetarian diet for countless generations.

- Seventh Day Adventists throughout the world whose religion discourages the eating of flesh.

- The Hunzas, who have thrived for centuries on an almost flesh-free diet.

Add to the above, countless health faddists and fitness freaks who are switching over to a vegetarian diet every year!

28. God made animals to be food for humans. So why should you raise a song and dance about it?

If this is indeed so, why should animals scream and howl in pain when they are slaughtered? Perhaps you will argue that they have not read the scriptures!

A holy man I know tells his disciple who still wants to eat meat, "Fine! But don't buy the meat. Kill the animal yourself, and eat him." Many of us continue to eat flesh only because someone else does all the killing and the bloodshed, and the meat is brought, beautifully prepared to your table!

CHAPTER TEN

MAKING THE RIGHT CHOICE

Naivedya:

I have set before you life and death, blessing and cursing:
Therefore choose life.

— Deuteronomy 30:19

Invocation:

Meat-eating and World Peace appear to be poles apart.
So long as animals and birds are slain to provide food
for man, we will not have peace on the face of this
earth. For, if a man kills an animal for food, he will not
hesitate to kill a fellow human being whom he regards
as his enemy. The root cause of world wars is ir-
reverence towards life. Wars will not cease until all killing
is stopped.

— J.P. Vaswani

Apertif:

Man is made or unmade by himself. By the right choice
he ascends. As a being of power, intelligence, and love,
and the lord of his own thoughts, he holds the key to
every situation.

— James Allen

✦ Starters ✦

Holidays should be times for deep reflection. Ponder these facts. More than 45 million turkeys are killed in the US every Thanksgiving day. More than 300 million are killed annually. Before they are mercilessly slaughtered they are kept in the most inhumane conditions, on the floors of dark, filthy sheds, a house of horors, where they walk through their own excrement, breathe ammonia filled air, and are cramped together so tightly they can't move or get away from one another. As a result there are numerous fights among normally peaceful individuals and they suffer from massive injuries and a variety of diseases. When one eats a turkey carcass they are eating a genetically engineered animal and also consuming pain and misery. To keep turkeys from injuring one another their toes and beaks are cut off with hot blades with no anesthetic or analgesic, and when their throat is slit many are still conscious. We know chickens feel empathy and there is every reason to believe that turkeys do too. I know no one would treat their dog like turkeys are treated from birth to their heinous road to death.

There are numerous tasty non-animal alternatives

and even if you don't think they're as yummy as a dead bird is it really asking too much to give up something that isn't a necessary part of your diet? I don't think so. In order to make changes in the way we live, including who, not what, we eat, we occasionally need to leave our comfort zones. By not turning a blind eye to the incredible suffering that turkeys experience and choosing to forgo eating them, you can add more compassion to the world. You can even adopt a turkey.

I urge everyone to try to make this simple change right now, for this coming holiday. I can't imagine you wouldn't feel better about yourself. Thank you for trying.

– Marc Bekoff, Professor Emeritus of Ecology and Evolutionary Biology at the University of Colorado, Boulder.

✦ Main Course ✦

Let me begin with the well known Vedic invocation: *Sarve Bhavantu Sukhinah: Sarve Santu Niramaya: Sarve Badhrani Pashyantu Maa Kashchid – Dukha Bhavbhaveta!*

May all beings be happy,

May all be healthy,

May people have the well-being of all in mind,

May no body suffer in any way.

May all, all beings be happy!

The shortest route to world peace and universal happiness, I believe, is through love, compassion, the spirit of caring and sharing and service. It is also the shortest and quickest route to God. The way of loving kindness is closely allied to the way of brotherhood, for we need to assert, again and again, "I am my brother's keeper!"

And who are our brothers? Our brothers and sisters are all those who suffer and are in need of help – men, women, birds and animals. We must become channels of God's mercy, help and healing, so that His love may flow out to them through us and our actions. When we become instruments of God's love, there is no limit to what we can accomplish. In God's divine plan, we can become the sanctuary of the weary and heavy-laden, the oppressed and exploited, all those creatures who suffer and are in pain; we can, with our efforts, become a source of sweet, refreshing waters in the wilderness that is this world.

There is a story in wide circulation about a question asked of Rabbi Hillel, a notable rabbi from the 1st century BC. Someone asked the rabbi to teach him everything about the Torah while standing on one foot. Rabbi Hillel responded: *"What is hateful to you, don't do unto your neighbour. The rest is commentary. Now, go and study."*

There is a simple question that all saints ask of us: How can we claim to love God if we do not love our fellow human beings? How can we call ourselves human beings if we watch our brothers and sisters suffering and struggling?

God cannot be satisfied with our adoration and devotion if they come only from our lips – for words and alphabets cannot make a prayer. It is our hearts and our own lives that must bear witness to our devotion, and what better way to achieve this than through the service of our fellow human beings and all creatures that breathe the breath of life?

We all have something to offer to the cause of universal peace!

Let us live with love and compassion, and we will make the world a better place!

How can I refrain from quoting those beautiful lines that have never failed to inspire me! "I shall pass through this life but once. Any good, therefore, that I can do Or any kindness that I can show to any fellow creature, Let me do it now. Let me not defer or neglect it, For I shall not pass this way again."

Don't hold back! Don't underestimate yourself and your abilities! Don't imagine that you cannot make a difference! We may feel that our effort is but a drop in the ocean, yet every drop counts in the ocean of service!

On an unforgettable day, Gurudev Sadhu Vaswani and a few of his devotees went walking by the river. It was a beautiful day, and a congenial mood prevailed among us, for I was privileged to be in that blessed fellowship.

All of sudden, a shadow seemed to fall on us. The Master was disturbed; pain and grief were reflected in his normally luminous glance.

We followed the direction of his eyes, and we saw what he had seen. A lone fisherman sat on the bank of the river, catching fish. He had already landed a few fish, which were put into an earthenware pot of water kept beside him.

The Master approached the fisherman and said to him, "Can you sell to me all the fish you have caught this morning?"

The man stared at Gurudev Sadhu Vaswani,

puzzled. To his experienced eyes, this was no average customer for fresh water fish. And anyway, why did he not come to the fish market where he would have a wide choice? And then, why did he want the entire catch of the morning? "Why do you want all my catch?" he asked, guardedly.

"Because," Gurudev Sadhu Vaswani said, "I would like to release the whole lot into the water."

"And what about my livelihood?" the man demanded.

"I do realise that you must earn your living, my friend," the Master said. "This is why I offer to buy the fish from you." "How much will you offer for this lot?" "Whatever you ask."

The fisherman decided to argue his case further. "Alright," he said, "Supposing you were to buy this lot from me and release them into the water, what difference will it make? I'm not the only fisherman here; there are hundreds of us. So you release five fish – five small fish into the water, what difference will it make?"

"May I show you?" the Master asked him gently. "Do show me sir," said the man. "I would like to see what difference it makes."

Gurudev Sadhu Vaswani asked one of us to offer the man twenty rupees, for the Master carried no money with him. The fisherman's eyes widened in surprise, for it was more than the few fish were worth!

"May I?" said Gurudev Sadhu Vaswani, gently lifting the small pot of water. He poured just a little of the water into the river, and out jumped one little fish. Oh, you should have seen the tiny creature frisk and play in the flowing waters! It seemed to know, instinctively, that it had managed to escape the jaws of death!

The fisherman stared at it, as did all of us. He had seen fish quirm and stiffen as he hauled them up from the river. This reversal of his daily process took his breath away! And the fish seemed to dance and swim merrily before his eyes!

"You see, it makes a great deal of difference to her," the Master said to him.

As he emptied the contents of the pot, five bright and lively fish repeated the joyous performance before our delighted eyes.

"You can make a difference," the Master repeated. Thus, it was that the Master showed us that every creature that breathes the breath of life loves life as much as we do. In our unthinking, selfish haste to exploit them, we fail to see the pain and cruelty we inflict on them.

Animal abuse is another form of cruelty to animals, and causing them unnecessary harm and suffering. Personally, I feel that factory farming and even animal testing are barbaric practices, unworthy of any evolved civilisation. For me, cruelty to animals is a moral issue.

There are people to speak up against all other forms of exploitation, and you will forgive me if I voice my support for the dumb and defenseless creatures. They have no press, no TV, no media, no spokesperson to voice their grievances. They need friends, they need spokespersons!

Have you ever spared a thought for the atrocities that are perpetrated on the animals day after day, in laboratories and in slaughterhouses? Have you thought of these creatures imprisoned in their tiny cages, deprived of light, fresh air and free movement, compelled to stand and live in their own filth? Have you thought of animals 'stunned' and then hung upside down in a line to have their throats slit? And after this appalling treatment, they are finally eaten up, consumed! And this nightmare goes on, day after day.

My friends, let me tell you, there will be no peace on earth until we stop the exploitation of animals, until we stop all killing!

Current civilisation, built as it is on the exploitation of the poor, and on the blood of the dumb, defenseless creatures, is crumbling beneath the burden of its own weight. The new civilisation that is to dawn, must be built on a nobler, worthier ideal. If civilisation is to endure, it must be built in a new spirit of reverence, in a new religion of reverence for all life.

Animal welfare is not enough! We must speak of animal rights! Men have their rights; have animals no rights? I believe, the time has come when all animal lovers must get together and formulate a charter of animal rights, a charter of man's duty towards the animal kingdom. I hope and pray that India, the country of the Buddha, Mahavira, and Sadhu Vaswani, will be among the first nations to pass on enactment giving rights to animals.

Every animal has its fundamental rights. And the very first right of every animal is the right to live! We cannot take away that which we cannot give! And since we cannot give life to a dead creature, we have no right to take away the life of a living one!

The time is come when we must decide once and for all that all types of exploitation must cease. We must recognise the moral inviolability of individual rights, both human and nonhuman. Just as black people don't exist as resources for white people, just as poor don't exist as resources for rich, just as women don't exist as resources for men, even so animals don't exist as resources for human beings! In the words of my Revered Master, Sadhu Vaswani, "No nation can be free, until its animals are free!"

The world cannot be at peace until all forms of exploitation cease!

According to the Hebrew Scriptures, humans are conceived as superior to all the rest of creation, which exists merely for his use and exploitation. However, according to Midrash, the method by which the ancient Jewish Rabbis investigated Scripture in order to make it yield laws and teachings that were not apparent in a surface reading – God is reported as saying to man: 'All that I have created has been for your sake; take care then not to spoil and destroy My world.' In other words, God put a restraint on man, enjoining him to care for the various orders of creation 'beneath' him. This envisages a hierarchy in creation, with the higher levels expected to exercise responsibility as stewards, guardians and caretakers.

At every step, in every round of life, we are given choices. There are always choices to be made, for God has given us the freedom to choose what we like, in the form of what has been called free will.

We can choose what we like! If we make the right choices, we will grow in health, happiness and vitality. If we make the wrong choice, we suffer from disease, loss of energy, loss of vitality, loss of creativity and loss of enthusiasm.

What will you choose?

If you make the right choice, the gift of a long, happy, healthy life is yours to enjoy.

Choose to accept God's love for you. He wants

you to live life to the fullest, not merely exist! Accept His infinite love, and you will find that power and vitality and positive vibrations flow into you.

It was an inspired poet who said, "We receive but what we give." When we offer our love to God, we receive His infinite love to us. When we offer ourselves and our life to Him, He makes our life blessed and beautiful! And loving God means loving all of His creation.

St. Francis prayed, "Bless all things that have breath: guard them all from evil!"

To us in India, this is expressed in the faith of the ancient *rishi* who urged us, "Look upon all sentient beings with kindly eyes!"

Gurudev Sadhu Vaswani lifted up his heart in prayer to the Lord of all Life with the words:

"O, Lord! Bless the birds: they sing the songs that purify our hearts and reveal the beauty and the mystery of life. O Lord! Protect the mild-eyed cow and the faithful dog and the honest horse and every beast and every worm that groaneth, from the cruel hand of man!"

Should your hands be among those cruel ones? Surely, you have the choice not to let them be cruel! These hands were given to us to bless, not to butcher; to help and heal, not to harm other creatures; to serve, not to slaughter!

Don't become the slave of your appetite; do not allow the slaughter of innocent animals to please your palate. Therefore, eat right, and also for all the right reasons. Choose good food, not for its taste or its appeal to the palate.

Food should be tasty and pleasant, of course. But that is not its primary purpose. We eat to live, we don't live to eat. Therefore, we must choose foods that enhance life and vitality. We must live and let live.

An ancient story tells us that the Angel of Food came before the Divine Presence, battered, exhausted, and severely downcast.

"I can't take it any more," he complained. "People abuse me, exploit me. There is no respect for me, no piety of the realisation that I am Your *prasadam* to men! Everyone indulges in excess. Never has there been such ill-treatment meted out to one of your gifts!"

The Lord smiled and said to him: "Those who abuse you and indulge in excess are destroying themselves!"

All diets choices have their consequences. Fast foods fill you up – but they will not sustain your health and vitality. Quick-fix foods that come in packets will give you chemicals and additives, but not much by way of nutrition or good taste. The food of violence, the flesh of dead animals may titillate your taste buds; but will leave you with a sense of guilt and waste!

'Dead' foods only make your stomach a grave yard for diseased carcasses.

Change your diet, and you will change your life for the better.

In this case, the difference between the right and wrong choice is the difference between life and death.

✦ *Food for Thought* ✦

For hundreds of thousands of years, the mutton stew in the pot has boiled up a resentment very hard to level. If you want to know why there are wars in the world, just listen to the haunting cries that come from a slaughter house at midnight.

The grief and hatred brewed up in a pot of meat stew is as deep as the ocean. It could never be fully described. The wars and massacres in the world are brought about by the convergence of the evil *karma* of living beings, causing beings to undergo retribution at the same time. If you listen carefully to the cries of misery coming from a slaughter-house in the middle of the night, you will realise the horror of the ceaseless killing that goes on in there.

Scientists have discovered that people who eat a great deal of meat tend to get cancer. This is because the resentful energy in the bodies of slaughtered animals accumulates in the bodies of those who eat meat and eventually turns into a harmful toxin. We should cut off this relationship of causes and effects with animals and stop the vicious cycle of creating offenses against cows, sheep, pigs, chickens, and other animals. Then we will gradually be able to lessen the inauspicious energy in the world.

– Venerable Master Hsuan Hua

Dessert

In June 1995, animal waste from abattoirs contained in an eight-acre lagoon in North Carolina burst through its dike, spilling approximately 22 million gallons of animal waste into the New River. The spill was twice the size of the Exxon Valdez oil spill, and reportedly killed fish along a 19-mile downstream area. This was the worst of six reported spills in the state during the summer of 1995.

– Environmental Concerns and the
Economics of Vegetarianism

SADHU VASWANI MISSION'S

www.sak.org.in

Kindly observe November 25
Sadhu Vaswani's birthday
as Meatless Day and Animal Rights Day